Why I Cook

Why I Cook

TOM COLICCHIO

with Joshua David Stein

ARTISAN

NEW YORK

Library of Congress Cataloging-in-Publication Data is on file.

ISBN 978-1-64829-128-9
ISBN 978-1-64829-489-1 (signed edition)

Design by Suet Chong

Artisan books may be purchased in bulk for business, educational, or promotional use. For information, please contact your local bookseller or the Hachette Book Group Special Markets Department at special.markets@hbgusa.com.

The publisher is not responsible for websites (or their content) that are not owned by the publisher.

The Hachette Speakers Bureau provides a wide range of authors for speaking events. To find out more, go to hachettespeakersbureau.com or email HachetteSpeakers @hbgusa.com.

Published by Artisan,
an imprint of Workman Publishing,
a division of Hachette Book Group, Inc.
1290 Avenue of the Americas
New York, NY 10104
artisanbooks.com

The Artisan name and logo are registered trademarks of Hachette Book Group, Inc.

Printed in China on responsibly sourced paper
First printing, September 2024

10 9 8 7 6 5 4 3 2 1

For my sons, Dante, Luka, and Mateo.
You are everything.

Contents

In loving memory of
Jerry Bryan
March 8, 1958–May 12, 2024

Silence

THERE'S NO SUCH THING as quiet in August on the North Fork of Long Island. The air vibrates with the humid thrum of summer, the shouts of kids' laughing calls from the pool, the chirp of crickets in the sycamores. The insects' sound reminds me of tickets spitting from a kitchen printer during a busy dinner service. I'm happy they're not. Tiki, my flat-coated retriever, nudges a stick against my legs, hoping I'll take the bait and throw. I'd like to, but there is work to do, as there always is when the sun is out. We have a kitchen garden, you see. A big one. Its demands, which change by the day, run me during these summer months, and to ignore them spells calamity. When my wife, Lori, and I bought the house in 2002, this garden was just a stretch of parched and patchy grass, too shadeless and sunny for play. I procrastinated for ten years before I got busy laying a dozen raised beds and filling them with vegetables and flowers for pollinators. Now, it's my passion. Weeds are poking up—a new crop since I went after them this morning. Eight or so varieties of tomatoes hang wantonly for picking. Blackberries grow to the size of a human thumb, taunting

---

me to get busy, even though I know I'll be pricked. And as I pick, plans form: Maybe a quick dice of this zucchini, tossed with the tuna we caught on the boat yesterday. These deep-purple eggplants will work with raisins and capers for caponata. The tomatoes need very little—sliced, they'll lay out nicely with the hand-pulled mozzarella I buy at Lombardi's. And on from there.

The cycle whereby a seed becomes a plant and then ultimately a food has been magical to me since I watched it up close in my grandpa Mike's driveway in early childhood. Grandpa had plants in five-gallon buckets growing against the red brick of our four-family home in Elizabeth, New Jersey. With a Marlboro hanging from his mouth (it never fell), he'd use his worker's fingers to gently coax a single tendril from the dirt. Mere weeks later, he'd be cutting back leaves. Why chop away so much? He explained that removing the excess would allow the precious energy and nutrients from sun and soil to be driven into the fruit. My first taste of agriscience.

At the height of the season, my grandfather's buckets ran amok with tomato plants, pepper bushes, and ropy zucchini vines. Here was Nature! But it's the tomatoes I remember best, if only because they were a staple food for us. Grandpa picked them, Grandma canned

My parents, with my grandparents, at their wedding in 1960

them, and we ate them in everything, all year long. There aren't too many things in the world that reward hard work, patience, and care as consistently or exuberantly as a tomato plant.

When I was a kid, my mother's father was a daily presence in my life, informing much of what I knew of men and manhood. He was a straight shooter, a cause-and-effect guy well suited to the reliable output of driveway gardening. He was strict and old guard; legend was he'd refused to let my mother and her sister out of the house as teenagers. She met my father in high school and—because that's how it worked in those days—they got married as soon as he left the service. (With a father like hers, there was no playing the field.) But my dad wasn't home much, so even after she married, Grandpa stayed a primary figure in my mother's life, and therefore in my brothers' and mine, too. He and my grandmother lived more or less next door, and our lives were woven together in a way that seems hard to imagine today. Grandpa would shuttle us around, since my mom didn't drive, and wait with a newspaper behind the wheel until it was time to drive us back home. It was he who took me out for bluefish or crabs at dawn in Barnegat Bay, sparking my lifelong romance with fishing. My grandmother, Esther, was loving and warm—on her good days. The rest of the time she seemed off her rocker—the clinical term then for what we now call bipolar—baking cakes with frantic energy or retreating into bleak stretches of dark inertia. My grandfather patiently weathered her storms, ate the cake, or quietly took over cooking duties when she was too low to get out of bed. Grandpa was square, but he was also creative and inventive. He kept tanks of bright tropical fish in the basement, next to his workshop. I'd spend hours down there with him, helping him repair anything and everything by the glow of those aquariums. Nothing was unsalvageable, not a television set on the fritz, not a lamp with wiring gone wrong. Nothing—and no one, it seemed—wasn't worth the work.

My father's father, Felix Colicchio, died when I was four, and my father was in a permanent state of feud with his mother, Olga, so I didn't know them as well. Felix and Olga had both been born in Vallata, a devout and earthquake-prone town in Italy's Campania, and had immigrated, separately, to the States, my grandfather in 1903 and my grandmother soon after. They met and married in Elizabeth and had five kids. My father was the youngest. I don't remember hearing much about my father's childhood, but we all knew that life for Felix and Olga and their children was hardscrabble. As a kid, my dad owned a single tiny toy truck, which he cherished his whole life. He and his siblings grew up hungry and fast.

Elizabeth is an industrial town nestled into northern New Jersey's historic manufacturing belt. It's best known for its shipping container port (one of the eastern seaboard's largest), the titanic Singer Sewing Machine plant (where Grandpa Felix worked), and (as Lori reminds me) for having produced that totem of young-adult fiction, Judy Blume, who went to school with my mom. Rumor was that Elizabeth had once been lovely, but by the 1970s there were few parks and green spaces, unless you counted the thatch of trees by the Elizabeth River that also grew old tires and retired refrigerators. Maybe that's why almost every Italian family I knew had a grandparent like mine, patiently coaxing vegetables and plants from small backyard patches of concrete, following the rhythms of their home country. Is that what has me out weeding in the mornings? Is it in my DNA?

I knew little of Elizabeth's history, but I could have easily rattled off its neighborhood ecology: The Poles lived in Frog Hollow, the Jews in Elmora. Italians largely lived in Peterstown, Black folks lived in the Port, and the professional class stuck to Westminster. My neighborhood, though, was a sort of non-neighborhood neighborhood right in the middle that didn't have a name. Our nearest neighbors were the Kauchauks, Wards, Donnegans, Slavinskys, and Jonokos, all second- or third-generation immigrant families like mine with a tenuous hold on the middle class. Despite the ethnic

Grandpa Mike and me on Barnegat Bay

diversity, the kids on our block were more alike than not: Our fathers all held blue-collar jobs. Our mothers took care of the home. Everyone was intertwined with grandparents, aunts, uncles, and cousins who doubled as our best friends and occasional enemies. Around dinnertime, the smells of pierogies, galumpkis, and boiled beef wafted out of houses, signaling to us kids that we'd need to wrap up our ball games in the street and head indoors. We'd trudge past our fathers who were sitting with a can of PBR watching the local news, kiss our mothers who hadn't sat down once all day, and take our places at the table. My own mother still wouldn't sit, hovering between stove and table as we ate. Today that bugs me, but back then that's simply how it was.

Another thing that simply was was my silent, brooding father, for whom I'm named. He kept to himself at home. He wasn't disinterested, exactly—it's just that my brothers and I, along with everything else within the walls of our two-bedroom apartment, were the province of my mother, and he left it to her.

For a time my father owned a barbershop, and then he worked as a correctional officer at the Union County jail. He was an occasional bookie and always a gambler, two other things I grew up taking for granted. It was only later that I became aware of the disruption and anxiety my dad's gambling caused my mother, or understood its pathology as an addiction. Back then, as far as I knew, this was yet another thing that men simply did. My father was passionate about local politics—a blood sport in North Jersey—and was an active and proud union member, even serving as head of the Policemen's Benevolent Association Union for a time. He could be funny and charismatic when he felt like it, with a biting wit. I always thought that if things had turned out differently for him, if a few of those bad bets had gone the other way, he could have made a great politician. Instead, he spent most of his adult life working an uninspiring job that offered him "twenty and out," i.e., a pension after twenty years of grim service. He may have been an officer of the jail, but he was also doing time.

My father avidly watched college football on Saturdays and pro on Sundays and Mondays, with an intensity I came to understand had less to do with the games and more to do with the cash he'd staked on their outcome. If I wanted to spend time with him, I watched, too. Father-son heart-to-hearts weren't his style, which was fine, because they weren't mine, either. I don't remember him ever saying that he loved me, but I never questioned that he did. He showed up at every basketball game. He even coached my baseball team, though I wasn't very good. He was up each morning at dawn to drive me to swim practice in his Cadillac Seville. Silent as he was, I knew that was love.

We never made conversation on those early-morning drives. He didn't ask about me or share his thoughts. It could be awkward, even oppressive, at times, but it nonetheless felt as normal to me as the cigarette smoke swirling between us, or riding shotgun without a seatbelt, or any of the countless things that would be alien to my own boys today. This was simply how I understood my father—and, by extension, men—to be. Quiet, sometimes simmering, occasionally volatile, but saving the best of themselves for a bigger, more consequential world to which we aspired but weren't yet invited.

Today I wonder what my father would have shared if I had known what to ask. Would he have told me how stifling it was to grow up dirt poor in the 1940s, on the same square blocks he'd always known, with few prospects and no clear path out? Would he have shared stories of being stationed in Germany in the mid-1950s, meeting people from all over for the first time in his life? Did that give him thoughts of seeing the world?

But he didn't talk, and he didn't invite me to, either. If he had, I imagine I would have told him about facing off against the nuns at St. Mary's who had had it already with me, the class clown. How they hit me for my smart mouth and inability to sit still, until the day I grabbed the ruler out of a Sister's hands and dared her to try it again (she didn't). I might have told him about how much I loved being out on the water at dawn with Grandpa Mike raking for clams. How I needed that calm, because three hormonal boys in one small bedroom was loud and chaotic and being the shortest kid in the class meant being ready to show you could fight at any moment, plus having the nuns on my case . . . Frankly, it was all kind of exhausting.

Then again, I don't know if I would have articulated any of that, even if he'd asked. These were simply the conditions of life, unremarkable. As was the constant scrapping with my brothers—Mike, fourteen months older than me, and Phil, four years younger. Mike had inches and twenty pounds on me, but I was fast and stealthy (as all younger brothers must be). Phil was young enough to go crying to our mom, but he rarely did, which earned him a few points. My mother would beg us to stop—she was losing her mind with the jousting, the tackling, the noise. She'd shout, "Wait until your father comes home!" and we'd laugh at her, though a small part of us feared the day it was more than just an empty threat.

If we were being particularly awful, my mother would force us to come along on her errands—a special circle of hell for a preteen boy. I can remember being compelled to sit at my cousin Patty's beauty salon once while my mother had her weekly appointment. I picked up a magazine from the stack by the hair dryers, bored before I even opened it. Under it was one I hadn't seen before, called *Cuisine*. Up to this point, I enjoyed helping out in the kitchen—mixing the Sunday meatballs, sometimes helping Grandma with her cakes—so it caught my eye.

On the cover was a portrait of an elderly Black woman and something about Cajun cooking, which I'd never heard of. This was long before Paul Prudhomme and K-Paul's Louisiana Kitchen, and the cuisine was still unknown to most of the country. I flipped to the article

Top, from left to right, my brothers Phil, Mike, and me, and, bottom, with our grandparents

and was immediately drawn in. The author traced the origins of this exotic-sounding cuisine—jambalaya, gumbo, boudin, andouille—that had been brought to Louisiana in the eighteenth century by French Acadians expelled from Canada and then synthesized with the West African cooking traditions of the region's enslaved population. The article described how the cuisine was further developed and refined by Black women working as domestics and cooks in the white homes of New Orleans, evolving into what became known as Creole cooking. This was the first time that I'd considered how food—what we ate—carries with it stories that could serve as a window into history, a subject I loved. American history sure wasn't taught that way at St. Mary's.

The article had a recipe at the end, accompanied by a full-page color photograph of a roasted eggplant, cut in half and hollowed out, stuffed with a roasted mixture of eggplant, rice, zucchini, onions, peppers, and shrimp. The dish was called Eggplant Pirogue, which sounded altogether like something else to me, but what did I care? Here was something actionable, something to do. "I can make this," I thought. With her fresh perm looking (to my eyes) exactly as it had when we walked in, my mother signaled she was ready to go. I asked my cousin Patty if I could take the magazine home with me and she agreed.

I went home and followed the recipe the best I could, serving it up to my family that night. It was the first meal I'd ever cooked, and it was a success, though a limited one. Unfortunately, the Eggplant Pirogue was just an appetizer—I would have had to read it all the way through to the end to know that. (Recipes were then, and still are, almost impossible for me to read from beginning to end.) When everyone finished their plates and looked up for more, I had to tell them we were all out. My mother, as she always did, saved me, ducking into our kitchen to make her go-to cavatelli with broccoli. But my dad weighed in in a way that he rarely did: with praise. "Not bad, Tom." That made an impression.

One day soon after, Dad came home from his job at the jail with a tall stack of books. "I found these in the library at work," he said. "I thought you'd like them." He plopped the books on the kitchen table: the austere black cover of *The New York Times Cookbook* by Craig Claiborne, the tattered beige *Joy of Cooking* by Irma S. Rombauer, *La Technique* by Jacques Pépin, with its black-and-white illustration of a lobster on the cover. The books must have been donated by a well-meaning Elizabeth housewife, though I wondered if she realized her intended beneficiaries didn't cook their own food. I was flattered that my father had been thinking of me out there in his larger world (though now that I'm a father, I know that verbal output to one's kid does not correlate to the real estate they take up in your head). Of the books, my favorite was Pépin's *La Technique*, because it was laid out like no other cookbook I'd ever seen: Each recipe was a series of thumbnail photos, walking the reader through the actions he described, which kept someone with the attention span of a gnat (me) engaged. Pépin's words in the foreword resonated: "Techniques matter more than recipes," he wrote. That made sense to me, and so did the instructions that came next: "Don't treat this book as a cookbook," he wrote, "treat it as an apprenticeship." And so I did. I started by developing basic knife skills, practicing on celery, which was cheap and plentiful. Once I mastered a mirepoix, I followed Pépin's instructions and learned how to make chicken stock, graduating from there to consommé, which was a good deal more involved, since it required clarifying the broth with egg whites. While my brothers were off doing homework, I was turning olives into rabbits and cream puffs into swans.

I'd be lying, though, if I said I swapped cooking for the usual teenage pursuits or thought of it as a career option. My brain simply didn't go there. It was 1977. Girls and partying occupied the largest part of my frontal lobe. My brother Mike and I ran with a wild, feral pack of friends and older cousins who impressed us with their criminality. We blasted Bruce's "Born to Run" (our anthem) over the car speakers, scored whatever we could get our hands on, and thought little about where it all would lead. Unlike my kids today, who live their lives with an expectation of college and an exciting future, at that age my friends and I were all id, chasing fun wherever it would present itself, consequences be damned. Maybe the lack of future planning was simply our adolescent brains, or maybe it was because subconsciously we all assumed adulthood was the end of the road, when we'd have to start down the plodding, soul-sucking road of our fathers—"twenty and out"—and so we'd better cram it all in now. I'm not sure, but I do know that it started to change one day—I must have been around sixteen—when my father casually remarked "Tom, you like food. Maybe you should become a chef. I think you'd be good at it." *He thought I'd be good at it.*

It's difficult to overstate the impact of those words. It seemed that my dad had been paying attention to my idiot shenanigans and think-ing about my future, even if I wasn't. And with this realization came another: that here was a man who had spent decades in a job he hated, who didn't want me to do the same.

Now, to be clear, I don't think my father (or anyone, yet) imag-ined the possibilities of what "chef" would come to mean in our cul-ture. To him, a chef was a tradesperson, like a mechanic or a barber. But that's beside the point: He wanted me to like what I did with my life, and maybe even feel pride in my work. *I think you'd be good at it.* That's the power of a father's words on a son's developing psyche: As he articulated what he saw, I could suddenly see it, too.

Who knows what "chef" even meant to me at sixteen? The one restaurant my family went to was Spirito's, an Italian joint kitty-corner to O'Brien's Field in Peterstown. Hilariously, I didn't even know it was a full-on restaurant for years, since we'd always gamely trooped into the bar behind my father, who'd grab a stool and leave us to entertain ourselves in a booth (I think I was in high school before I glimpsed the dining room). Spirito's may have been humble (pic-ture faux wood paneling and red Naugahyde seats), but that's not to say that it wasn't great. Since its opening in 1932, Spirito's had been run by three generations of the same family and the menu was old-school and ironclad. Marinara, marsala, saltimbocca, stuffed quahogs. With all those options, though, our family's order never wavered: a plate of antipasti, some Italian provolone ("Make sure it's imported!" my dad would insist), and the veal cutlets with sauce. Never the veal parmigiana. Years later I took Lori there on one of our first dates and that's what we ordered. Why mess with a good thing?

On the way to the men's room at Spirito's I could glimpse the kitchen—the first professional one I'd seen. There was nothing romantic or heroic about it. The light was hard and bright and fell on stainless-steel counters, a tile floor, and a few tired-looking guys who resembled merchant marines in their white pants and porters' shirts. One old guy stood over a huge blackened stove, its eight burners each occupied by aluminum stockpots and sauté pans so beat up they looked like artifacts. Rounding out the space was a salamander (a long broiler), whose intense heat turned the air around it wavy and distorted, and a menacing deep fryer, roiling with oil. A middle-aged pizzaiolo stabbed his wooden peel into a blackened pizza oven, with a stack of empty pizza boxes waiting at his elbow. It was a far cry from the kitchens I would later work in or build myself, but mysterious and intimidatingly professional nonetheless.

Did I peek into the kitchen at Spirito's after my father's suggestion and view those old-timers differently in some way? Try to picture myself practiced and hardened like them one day? I don't remember. I also don't remember my father talking much further with me about it because, well, he'd said his piece, and now it was up to me.

2

The Gran Centurions

DON'T LET THE FANCY NAME fool you; the Gran Centurions Swim Club in Clark, New Jersey, was a decidedly blue-collar affair. It catered to North Jersey Italian Americans who didn't have places down the shore or for whom Atlantic City was too far away. You could spend all day there, letting the vinyl straps on the chairs imprint onto your body, playing Marco Polo in the pool, or shuffleboard or Ping-Pong, while your mother and aunts gossiped over gin rummy and cigarettes. My family had been early members of the club, joining with other families to put up the bond for its construction.

Come summer, my grandfather would drop off my mom and us boys at the club in the morning, and my father would join us there later, after work. By that point we'd be well chlorinated, nut brown, and spent. After 5 p.m. there would be an influx of dads, each of whom, like a free electron, would find his wife and kids. Together they'd make their way into the club's bar, or toward the barbecues, or to the snack shack on the pool deck that did brisk business in cheeseburgers and hot dogs.

Like many swim clubs in Jersey, Gran Centurions had a swim team that would compete with other local clubs. The big race was held on the Fourth of July. When I was around eight or nine, my dad suggested that I enter the contest in his usual succinct way: "Go in and race." I was doubtful. I was small for my age and, as I sized up the competition—bigger glistening boys in red Speedos, puffed up with confidence—not hopeful. But I jumped into the pool anyway and swam as hard as I could. I won the race by five lengths. When I heaved myself out, dripping and incredulous, the coach made a beeline for me. And just like that, I was on the swim team. That season I didn't lose a single race.

In the water, I could do no wrong. Freestyle, breaststroke, butterfly, backstroke. As I cut through the water, the mechanics of my body in suspension, the balance of exertion and breath, made sense. After a summer of winning races, I entered that fall brimming with confidence.

It was short-lived. Up until then I had been a decent student at St. Mary's. I was a quick reader, thanks in part to my mother's diligence with a speed-reading contraption she'd purchased for me and my brothers. Schoolwork came easily to me, and being a good student meant I was more or less a good kid.

Me (center) when I was still smart

That all came to an end in third grade. Suddenly, tasks that had felt easy before grew chewier, or even at times impossible. During tests, even though I knew the answers, I would seize up and leave the page nearly blank. I couldn't sit still. I had never been a monklike model of repose—what kid is?—but now I felt an overwhelming internal restlessness to move, to fidget, to stand and sharpen a pencil, anything. My attention, never rapt, would flee in unexpected directions, like a spooked fish or a startled horse. It would be captured at the periphery, by a squirrel on the window ledge, a friend's dropped pencil, the cool way buttons were sewn onto a sleeve—it didn't take much. I found I could make people laugh, so I leaned into that and became the class clown. The nuns, those paragons of grace and forbearance, arranged stern meetings with my parents. I was clearly bright, as they saw it, so the problem must lie with my character.

The gap between what I wanted to do and what I could actually pull off widened, and with it my inner noise grew. Tasks appeared as if on a distant shore, separated from me by a wide, rapidly moving river. I couldn't figure out how to get there—which stones to jump on, or how to build a bridge—and an unfamiliar anxiety took shape. Until now I had always thought of myself as a smart kid. Now I began to wonder if I had been wrong all along. Cracks began to form in my self-confidence, which only made the paralysis worse, a bad feedback loop if ever there was one. My grades took a dive, and my parents were called in to school yet again to discuss the problem of me. I'd resolve to do better but couldn't seem to pull it off.

To compensate, I doubled down on antics. I became a master at back talk. "Tommy," my algebra teacher would say, "can you solve for x?" "Yeah, I could," I'd say, "but I don't want to." The nuns were not amused. St. Mary's encouraged a change of scenery (they threw me out), so after freshman year I transferred to Elizabeth High. Things were no better there. In fact, they were arguably worse, because no one remembered me from when I was smart. By fourteen, my transformation was complete. Once your voice deepens and you start to shave, you're no longer the class clown; now you're something more serious: a bad kid.

Looking back, it's laughably clear that I was struggling with ADHD. Though the disorder had first been named in 1902 (described in manuals as "an abnormal defect of moral control in children"), in the 1970s no one thought to get kids like me checked out medically.

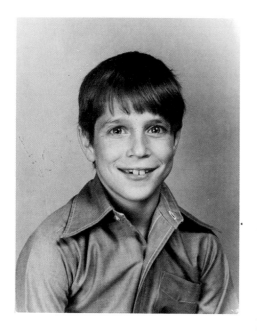

Even if they had, a diagnosis would have been unlikely. Outwardly I seemed fine. I could be impulsively gregarious, earning me friends, and I eventually figured out how to scrape by with Cs and low Bs. But inside I was confused, frustrated, and sad. A part of me still remembered that I used to be a smart kid, even if no one else did.

I don't know how much I registered the doubt and anxiety I was feeling at the time, but I can tell you exactly when and how I learned to press the pause button. At thirteen, I rolled my first joint, smoked it, and *voilà*! Bad feelings gone. Without the benefit of a therapist or Ritalin, I began to self-medicate. In the late 1970s—especially if you had wild older cousins, as I did—drugs of every stripe and purpose were easy to find. For a time I turned to mescaline, which made everything funny and loose, as did acid, which made listening to music a transcendental experience. I discovered I liked the state of being high. I liked how the world slowed down and flowed lazily by. Was this because I needed a way to calm the mental static caused by ADHD, because I was struggling with depression and frustration, or just because I was bored, undersupervised, and looking for kicks? The answer is yes.

I was still on the swim team, but predictably, this experimentation didn't mesh well with 5 a.m. swim practices, so I gradually blew them off, effectively ending my star career on the swim team. After St. Mary's kicked me out, though, I had another shot at it—Elizabeth High had a pool and a swim team, so I gave it another go. But this time, the same kids from Westfield and Cranford that I'd been beating in races for years were crushing me. The gap between the swimmer

I'd been (when I practiced) and the swimmer I was now was too wide, and it didn't seem like I could catch up. My already fragile self-esteem took another hit, adding to my disappointment in myself.

I craved being good at something and turned my focus outward, sometimes recklessly. Elizabeth wasn't a dangerous city in the same way as Trenton or Newark, but it was the kind of place where, if you were looking for trouble, it was easily found. This was the tail end of the golden era of the New Jersey mob, led by Sam "the Plumber" DeCavalcante in Trenton and by John Riggi in Elizabeth, who was married to my father's cousin. My family's connection was liminal at best, but there was always some minor racket to earn a few extra bucks. Items "fell off trucks" to be peddled at a discount. Uncles could arrange no-show jobs on construction sites. The casual acceptance of general grift led some of the kids I grew up with down darker paths, ending in prison. Others died. In this environment and in the head I was in, I could easily have found my own hustle and one day followed them off that cliff.

But—just as it had with its swim team—the Gran Centurions had unexpected plans for me. Don, the guy who ran the snack shack, needed help. I was fourteen and needed a job. Don hired me initially to work the cash register and scoop ice cream while he worked the grill. After a few days, we switched. It didn't matter that I had never cooked outside my own home before, because this was barely cooking. The burgers were premade and frozen. The chicken tenders were pre-fried and frozen. The french fries were poured straight from four-pound bags into the fryer, frozen. And the hot dogs were hot dogs, impossible to ruin. The closest thing to actual cooking was pressing two slices of buttered Wonder bread with a slice of Kraft cheese on the griddle for our famous Gran Centurions Grilled Cheese.

We arranged for Don to pick me up in the mornings for the fifteen-minute drive to Clark. The first thing I noticed was that the inside of his beat-up Datsun reeked of pot. I considered that a good sign but, out of propriety, said nothing and neither did he. Soon enough, the charade seemed pointless, especially when I saw him cupping a joint, so I asked, "Don, you want to share that?" He hesitated, as wonts a proper adult, then shrugged and handed it over. From that point, Don and I fell into an easy rhythm. He'd pick me up in the mornings, we'd get high before picking up provisions at ShopRite, and we'd arrive at the Gran Centurions around 11 a.m. Don worked the register while I moved between grill, griddle, and a couple of fryers, setting up. We'd roll open the gate and greet our public around noon (there was always a line) and work until the lunch rush subsided around, say, 3 p.m. I was off until 5 p.m., at which point I'd return and prepare for the nightly march of the fathers and the consequent dinner rush.

The snack shack was hot, smoky, smelly, greasy, and cramped, and I loved it. Standing at the grill barefoot, bare chested, tossing my long hair out of my eyes, I felt a sense of mastery over everything in my reach. The flattop, the fryer, it all made sense to me. Each new order Don called out, no matter how rapid-fire, seamlessly integrated in my mind into the orders that were already underway. I felt none of the anxiety a blank piece of paper in school could elicit, nothing but a calm sense of responding to incoming information in real time. I quickly developed muscle memory and an ear for the shifting sizzle of the fryer oil, telling me when to pull up the basket of fries. I could intuit when a grilled cheese was just at the right side of burnt and get a bun toasted at the corresponding moment its patty was ready. I was awash in a sense of competence and ease, that good feeling that comes from always knowing what to do next. It was like the old me—the real me—was back. I put that feeling in my pocket and carried it with me. It was worth more than the cash Don paid me under the table every week.

As the summer wore on, my ambitions grew. I got it in my head that I could create recipes from scratch, and Don went along with it. He let me buy minute steaks and racks of ribs. The grilled cheese was already our bestseller, but I worked on making it better. I dispensed with the frozen patties and bought ground beef, spicing it first and forming my own neat patties. I made my own barbecue sauce using ketchup and apricot jam. Word got around. Soon we branched out and started catering picnics for swim club members. My mother had bought me subscriptions to a few cooking magazines by then, so I must have been drawing from those, but also I was experimenting with ideas of my own; they were simple, but they were mine, and sometimes they were even good. The line at the snack shack grew longer, Don was happy, and best of all, I was growing. Without even intending to, we had transformed a mediocre concession stand into perhaps the best poolside snack shack in all of Union County. More importantly, I had found my lane.

Fall
Recipes

A Salad of Radicchio, Fennel, and Pear

In the fall, I can't get enough bitter Italian greens: Trevisano and Castelfranco radicchio, among others. I tend to like bitter flavors, which is why I'm a fan of chicories and Negronis, too. In this salad, the bitter greens combined with sweetness and acid works well in your mouth. For a bit of added earthiness and crunch, top the salad with some walnuts, if you feel inclined.

Serves 8

VINAIGRETTE
¼ cup honey vinegar (preferably Lindera Farms Honey Vinegar) or apple cider vinegar

2 tablespoons finely chopped shallot

Kosher salt and freshly ground black pepper

¾ cup extra-virgin olive oil

SALAD
8 cups (9 ounces) torn bitter greens, such as Treviso, Castelfranco, or dandelion

1 Bartlett pear, thinly sliced on a mandoline

1 fennel bulb, thinly sliced on a mandoline

Kosher salt and freshly ground black pepper

1 cup toasted walnuts (optional)

Make the vinaigrette: In a small bowl, mix the vinegar with the shallot. Season with salt and pepper. Slowly whisk in the olive oil until a cohesive dressing comes together. Taste and season with more salt if needed.

Assemble the salad: Place the bitter greens, pear, and fennel in a large bowl. Add the vinaigrette and gently toss. Season with salt and pepper. Top the salad with the toasted walnuts, if using, and serve.

The Dish That Launched a Thousand Brussels Sprouts

These days, Brussels sprouts are everywhere on restaurant menus. That's a good thing. When deep-fried and tossed with fish sauce—how they invariably appear—they're little bombs of flavor and texture. When we opened Craft, however, Brussels sprouts were a rarity on restaurant menus. No one wanted them. No one made them, at least not professionally. They were derided for their flavor, for their texture, for everything—so much so that they were a cliché of what you *didn't* want to eat. And then, at Craft, we started gently tossing them in rendered bacon fat and aromatics until their delicate flavor commingled with the richness of the bacon. People took notice and they began to sell, becoming one of our most popular sides. Soon, they began to spread to other menus, where methods of preparing them grew wider and more varied. (I am not, by the way, taking sole credit for popularizing Brussels sprouts, but like Edison bulbs and Chilewich place mats, there was a hockey stick upward after Craft.) But this, the original preparation, is still one of my favorite recipes and on regular rotation at home.

Serves 4

2 tablespoons extra-virgin olive oil, plus more for drizzling
6 ounces slab bacon, roughly chopped
1 small white onion, sliced
Kosher salt

2 pounds Brussels sprouts, trimmed and halved
¾ teaspoon fresh thyme leaves, plus 2 full sprigs thyme
Freshly ground black pepper

In a large sauté pan, heat the olive oil over medium heat until shimmering. Add the bacon and cook, stirring occasionally, until the fat is rendered and the bacon starts to crisp, about 5 minutes. Add the onion and season with salt. Cook together until the onion starts to soften, about 5 minutes.

(recipe continues)

Add the Brussels sprouts slowly in batches, so as not to overwhelm the pan, and season with salt. Add ¼ cup water and cook together, stirring occasionally, for 5 to 6 minutes. Add the thyme leaves and season with salt and pepper. Continue cooking until the Brussels sprouts start to become tender, 7 to 10 minutes.

Add the 2 sprigs of thyme and cook until the Brussels sprouts are soft and just starting to brown, 4 to 5 minutes. Taste and season with more salt and pepper and a drizzle of oil to finish.

Note: You can add small amounts of water if the Brussels sprouts start to stick to the pan, but don't add too much as you don't want them steaming in water.

Many Roasted Fall Squashes

There's little more I love to do in the autumn than wander around a farmers' market, admiring the many shapes, sizes, and colors of squash: the statuesque butternut squash, the squat red kuri, the pleated exterior of the Koginut. This dish is a celebration of that wide array. Keep the squash sliced—as opposed to diced—so you can see the beautiful curve of the vegetable. Use this recipe as a guideline, but do as I do and experiment with the different varieties of squash. Because each squash has a subtly different flavor and texture, the cooking times vary. Try cooking each variety separately and then tossing them together at the end, keeping in mind that the size and thickness affect cooking times. (To test for doneness: Pierce the squash with a metal cake tester. If it pierces easily, the squash is finished.)

Serves 4 to 6 as a side

4 to 5 tablespoons extra-virgin olive oil, plus more as needed

2 to 3 pounds assorted fall squash, such as butternut, Honeynut, Koginut, red kuri, or delicata, seeded and cut into slices ¼ inch thick

10 to 12 fresh sage leaves

Kosher salt and freshly ground black pepper

1 medium fennel bulb, shaved, fronds reserved for garnish

Juice of ½ lemon

In a large sauté pan, heat 2 to 3 tablespoons of the olive oil. Working in batches (so as not to crowd the pan), add the pieces of squash and sage leaves to the pan. Season with salt and pepper. Gently pan-roast the squash on both sides until lightly browned, 3 to 4 minutes per side. Remove to a plate and set aside. Repeat with the remaining squash, adding more olive oil as needed between batches. Remove the sage leaves when finished. (You can cook all the squash ahead of time.)

In a small bowl, toss the fennel with 2 tablespoons olive oil and the lemon juice. Season with salt and pepper to taste.

Transfer the squash to a platter and top with the dressed fennel and fennel fronds. Season with salt and pepper and serve.

Possibly the Best Grilled Cheese You'll Ever Have

Like many other dads, I make a lot of grilled cheese sandwiches for the kids. This one started as a way to use the mozzarella from Lombardi's Love Lane Market, an Italian deli in Mattituck that makes the world's best fresh mozz. Paired with 'nduja, a peppery spreadable Italian sausage, the grilled cheese essentially becomes a spicy pizza. It's decadent for sure, but the spice of the 'nduja cuts through the richness of the mozzarella. As always, but here especially, low and slow heat is important. It's the key to developing a nice crust on the bread, while also melting the cheese.

Makes 2 sandwiches

2 tablespoons extra-virgin olive oil

½ pound fresh mozzarella cheese, thinly sliced

4 thick slices peasant bread (see Note)

3 ounces soft 'nduja

4 tablespoons unsalted butter

Pour 1 tablespoon of the olive oil into a heavy-bottomed skillet and set over medium-low heat.

Layer the mozzarella slices on 2 pieces of the bread. Layer the 'nduja on the other 2 slices of bread.

Add 1 slice of mozzarella bread and 1 slice of 'nduja bread *open face* to the pan. Add 2 tablespoons of the butter to the pan. Cook for 2 minutes. Cover the pan and cook (still open face) for another 2 to 3 minutes, until the cheese is melted. Remove the hot melted slices from the pan and immediately flip them together to make a sandwich. Slice the sandwich in half crosswise.

Wipe the pan clean and repeat the process to make the second sandwich and serve immediately.

Note: Any bread will do, but I prefer one without a heavy sourdough flavor.

Frittata Like My Grandfather Used to Make

Whenever my grandfather took me fishing, he'd make us a pepper and onion frittata for lunch. The smell of peppers and onions frying still instantly brings me back to those predawn moments in his kitchen. To this day, when I go fishing, this is what I make, not just for nostalgia's sake but because it keeps so well and tastes delicious at room temperature. Be careful when you add the eggs that the pan is not ripping hot; otherwise the eggs will brown and become tough.

Serves 6 to 8

2 tablespoons extra-virgin olive oil

2 red bell peppers, thinly sliced

1 yellow bell pepper, thinly sliced

Kosher salt and freshly ground black pepper

1 small red onion, thinly sliced

12 large eggs, whisked

Preheat the oven to 350°F.

Pour the olive oil into a large ovenproof nonstick pan and place over medium heat. Add the bell peppers to the pan and season with salt and black pepper. Cook, stirring occasionally, until soft, 5 to 7 minutes. Add the onion, tossing together with the peppers, and cook until the onion is translucent, another 5 to 7 minutes. Season with salt and black pepper.

Once the vegetables are soft, increase the heat to high. Season the eggs with salt and black pepper and pour them into the pan. Transfer the pan to the oven. Bake until the top is lightly golden brown and the eggs are set, 15 to 20 minutes.

Remove from the oven and let rest for 5 minutes. Place a large plate on top of the pan and then invert. Cut into wedges and serve.

Storage: The frittata will keep covered in the refrigerator for up to 2 days; I think it's even better on day two.

Bucatini with Puntarelle, Black Olives, and Anchovies

Here the salty/umami punch of the combination of black olives, anchovies, and bitter puntarelle is softened by the pasta and sweetened by the garlic. If you, for some reason, don't want the pasta, simply omit it. If you want to make it sweeter, add some golden raisins. The puntarelle is perfect on its own. But any way you make it, be sure to add the anchovies and olives at the last minute. You don't want the anchovies to be cooked, which drastically changes their flavor.

Serves 4

Kosher salt

2 heads puntarelle

½ cup extra-virgin olive oil

2 red torpedo onions or small red onions, halved and sliced

2 small fennel bulbs, halved, cored, and sliced

1 head garlic, cloves separated and sliced

1 teaspoon crushed Calabrian chile pepper, or more to taste

Freshly ground black pepper

1 pound bucatini pasta

One 2-ounce tin anchovy fillets, chopped

½ cup oil-cured black olives, pitted and crushed

Bring a large pot of salted water to a boil over high heat for the pasta.

Meanwhile, fill a bowl with cold water. Remove the outer leaves of the puntarelle and cut the inner leaves into roughly 3-inch lengths. Cut the thicker stems into thin strips and transfer to the bowl of water.

In a large pot, heat the oil over medium heat. Add the onions, fennel, garlic, and Calabrian chile. Season with salt and black pepper. Cook, stirring occasionally, until the onions and fennel are soft, 5 to 7 minutes (reduce the heat to low if they are cooking too quickly).

(recipe continues)

Drain the puntarelle well and add to the pot. Toss to coat with the vegetables and cook, stirring occasionally, until the puntarelle is soft, 4 to 7 minutes. Taste to check the seasoning.

Meanwhile, add the bucatini to the boiling water and cook until al dente according to the package directions.

Reserving 1 cup of the pasta water, drain the bucatini and add to the pot with the vegetable mixture. Stir well, adding small amounts of pasta water until the sauce coheres and reaches a silky consistency.

Remove from the heat, stir in the anchovies and olives, and serve.

My Mother's Pasta with Broccoli . . . Not Really

My mother made a version of this cavatelli with broccoli almost every week of my childhood. I never once saw her use a measuring cup. She used her eyes, checking whether the dish looked "right" or not. She wouldn't have put it this way, but what my mother was looking for was ratios. Specifically, how much broccoli there was compared to the pasta. This amount came not from a recipe but from years of feedback from the Colicchio boys. (This broccoli-forward recipe is how I like it. Mike, my brother, prefers less broccoli but this is my book, not his.) So my advice is not to get hung up on the amounts of this or any recipe. Want less broccoli? Okay. Use two crowns. Want to add some chickpeas? Great. Do you want more chickpeas than broccoli or more broccoli than chickpeas or for them to be equally important? It's up to you.

Serves 4

Kosher salt
1 pound orecchiette, cavatelli, or other pasta shape
2 to 3 broccoli crowns, roughly chopped into small pieces
1 head garlic, cloves separated and thinly sliced

½ cup extra-virgin olive oil
¾ cup freshly grated pecorino cheese
Freshly ground black pepper
1 teaspoon crushed Calabrian chile pepper (optional)

Bring a large pot of generously salted water to a boil over high heat. Add the pasta and cook according to the package instructions. About 5 minutes before the end of the cooking time, add the broccoli to the pasta pot and give it a stir. Continue to cook the pasta and broccoli together. In the last minute of cooking, add the sliced garlic to the pot with the pasta and broccoli. Reserving 1 cup of the pasta water, drain the pasta, broccoli, and garlic and return to the pasta cooking pot.

(recipe continues)

Set the pasta pot over low heat. Add the olive oil, a splash of the reserved pasta water, and ½ cup of the pecorino. Toss together, adding more pasta water as needed to create a saucy consistency. Season with a good amount of black pepper and salt and add the Calabrian chile (if using). Garnish with the remaining pecorino and more black pepper.

Not Imitation Crab Rice

Crab rice, along with pasta with broccoli (page 39), was on my mother's short list of go-to dishes. Hers was made with the "crab sticks" they sold at the store—never the fresh crabs my grandfather and I caught, because those were destined for gravy—and lots and lots of butter. My version of crab rice is a little different but definitely inspired by what I grew up eating. I use fresh jumbo lump crab and start by sweating finely diced vegetables to form the base layer of flavor.

Serves 4 to 6

1½ cups Carolina Gold rice
¼ cup extra-virgin olive oil
1 small carrot, finely diced
¼ fennel bulb, finely diced
½ red onion, finely diced
1 celery stalk, finely diced
1 jalapeño, finely diced
1 garlic clove, minced
Kosher salt and freshly ground
    black pepper

2¼ cups chicken stock
2 tablespoons unsalted butter
8 ounces fresh jumbo lump
    crabmeat, drained and picked
    through
1 cup fresh parsley leaves,
    chopped
1 cup fresh cilantro leaves,
    chopped

Rinse the rice in several changes of cool water until the water runs clear. Drain and set aside.

In a large sauté pan, heat the olive oil over medium heat until shimmering. Add the carrot, fennel, red onion, celery, jalapeño, and garlic. Season with salt and pepper. Cook the vegetables, stirring occasionally, until they begin to soften, 4 to 5 minutes.

Stir in the rice and cook until evenly coated in the oil and lightly toasted, 1 to 2 minutes. Add the chicken stock and butter and season with salt and pepper. Bring to a boil over high heat. Once the stock boils, reduce the heat to low and cover the pot. Simmer until the rice is cooked through and the liquid has evaporated, about 15 minutes.

(recipe continues)

Remove from the heat and let stand for 5 minutes, then uncover the pot and add the crabmeat and herbs. Fluff with a fork and season to taste. Serve.

Storage: Leftover crab rice can be stored for 2 or 3 days covered in the fridge.

My (Latest) One-Pot Roast Chicken

Every cook has a roast chicken recipe, and this is mine. Sometimes. The truth is that this recipe is ever changing, depending on what's in season or what I have in the fridge. In the summer, I might use zucchini, sun-dried tomatoes (or roasted fresh ones), or Japanese eggplant. In the winter, I might use butternut squash or apple or nearly any other firm vegetable. (Soft ones get too mushy.) Regarding the chicken, it's important that the bird be dry before going into the pan. If you have time, place the chicken on a sheet pan skin-side up and refrigerate uncovered for at least a couple of hours (or even better, overnight). This will help dry out the bird, which will result in crispier skin.

Serves 4 or 5

¼ cup extra-virgin olive oil
1 whole chicken (3½ to 4 pounds), cut into 8 pieces (2 thighs, 2 drumsticks, and 2 breasts cut in half) and patted dry
Kosher salt
5 or 6 small Yukon Gold potatoes, halved
1 large fennel bulb, outer layer discarded, cored, and cut into ¾-inch wedges
1 red onion, cut into ¾-inch wedges
Freshly ground black pepper
3 Jimmy Nardello peppers, or 1 large red bell pepper, sliced

½ teaspoon fennel seeds
10 to 12 sprigs fresh thyme, plus more (optional) for garnish
2 sprigs fresh rosemary, plus more (optional) for garnish
1 large leek, white and light-green parts only, halved lengthwise and cut crosswise into 2-inch lengths
2 small lemons, thinly sliced
2 garlic cloves, sliced, plus 1 whole head, halved horizontally
2 tablespoons sherry vinegar

Preheat the oven to 400°F.

In a large Dutch oven, heat the olive oil over medium heat until shimmering. The pan does not have to be screaming hot.

(recipe continues)

45

Make sure the chicken is dry. Season the chicken generously with salt and add the dark meat pieces to the Dutch oven in a single layer skin-side down. Do not put in the smaller breast pieces first as they'll cook faster; add them a few minutes later. (If your pan isn't large enough to fit all the chicken in a single layer, you can brown the chicken in batches.)

Then leave them alone. Brown the chicken on all sides; try not to check it too often, but don't let it burn. Once browned, turn the pieces over to the other side. At this point, the chicken does not need to be fully cooked through. The whole process should take between 20 and 25 minutes. Remove the chicken from the pan and transfer the pieces to a plate.

Add the potatoes to the pan, followed by the fennel and onion, being careful not to overcrowd the pan too quickly. Season with salt and black pepper as you go. Add the Nardello peppers and fennel seeds. Gently toss the vegetables with a wooden spoon, adding ¼ cup water if necessary to deglaze the pan. Add the thyme and rosemary.

On the stovetop, pan-roast until the vegetables are softened and browned, 15 to 20 minutes.

Add the leeks and mix everything together. Season again with salt and black pepper. Stir in the lemon slices, sliced garlic, garlic head, and vinegar. Cook for 2 to 4 additional minutes on the stovetop as the vegetables just start to braise.

Place the chicken pieces, skin-side up, on top of the vegetables and transfer to the oven. Roast until the chicken is golden brown and cooked through, 15 to 20 minutes.

Season with salt and black pepper, garnish with fresh herbs, if desired, and serve.

Seared Scallops with Cabbage, Apples, and Leek

I had this recipe pictured in my mind before I ever made it. The dish is built around the beautiful sea scallops we get on Long Island. The cabbage, apples, and leeks each earn their place by bringing their own subtle hue of sweetness. During the summer, I make this with mushrooms. In winter, I pair the scallops with some winter citrus and olive oil, and maybe pistachios.

Serves 4

6 tablespoons extra-virgin olive oil

1 leek, white part only, sliced into half-moons

Kosher salt

1 small head green cabbage, sliced or shredded

1 small carrot, finely diced

Freshly ground black pepper

1 red apple, finely diced

½ teaspoon caraway seeds

1 tablespoon unsalted butter

¼-inch knob fresh ginger, finely diced

12 large diver or jumbo sea scallops

In a large sauté pan, heat 3 tablespoons of the olive oil over medium-low heat until shimmering. Add the leek and a pinch of salt. Cook until softened, 1 to 2 minutes. Add the cabbage and carrot and season with salt and pepper. Stir together and cook for 3 to 4 minutes. Add the apple and caraway seeds, stirring together, and cook until the cabbage is slightly wilted and just beginning to caramelize, about 5 minutes. (Do not let it burn!)

Keeping the heat low, season with salt and pepper, add the butter and ginger, and stir until the butter is melted, 2 to 3 minutes. Remove from the heat. Season to taste.

Line a plate with paper towels and keep near the stove. Pat the scallops dry and season with salt. Using a sharp paring knife, score both sides of the scallops in a crosshatch pattern. In a clean sauté pan, heat the remaining 3 tablespoons olive oil over medium heat until shimmering. Add the scallops, being careful not to crowd the pan. Sear for 4 to 5 minutes, then flip and cook for a few seconds more on the other side. Remove the scallops and place them on the paper towels to drain.

To serve, divide the cabbage salad among four plates. Top with the scallops and serve immediately.

Pork Chops with Cherry Peppers and Potatoes

Pork chops with cherry peppers was a dish my mother made for me when I was growing up, one that was in frequent rotation. I didn't think too much about it, but as I got older, whenever I would have pork chops, I found myself thinking "cherry peppers would be great with that." My mom was onto something. The combination makes a simple one-pot dish that nevertheless perfectly balances the fattiness of the pork with acid and heat from the peppers.

Serves 2 to 4

7 tablespoons extra-virgin olive oil, plus more as needed

5 or 6 small yellow potatoes, cut into slices ⅛ inch thick

Kosher salt

1 pound fresh cherry peppers

1 small red onion, sliced

3 small fresh Fresnos or other fresh hot chiles

1 tablespoon sliced garlic, plus 2 whole cloves, roughly chopped

4 or 5 fresh sage leaves

½ cup white wine vinegar

2 bone-in pork chops, 1 inch thick

Freshly ground black pepper

Preheat the oven to 375°F.

In a medium sauté pan, heat 2 tablespoons of the olive oil over medium heat. Add the potatoes in a single layer, being careful not to crowd the pan. If your pan is too small, you can cook these in batches, adding another tablespoon or so of oil as you go. Season the potatoes with salt and sear until browned on both sides, 3 to 4 minutes per side. Remove the cooked potatoes to a plate and set aside. Discard the oil remaining in the pan.

Return the pan to medium heat and add 3 tablespoons of the olive oil. Once it is shimmering, add the cherry peppers, onion, and Fresno chiles and cook until softened, 7 to 10 minutes.

(recipe continues)

Add the sliced garlic and 2 sage leaves and stir until fragrant, about 1 minute. Pour in the vinegar and season with salt. Continue to cook until most of the liquid has reduced, 3 to 4 minutes. Remove the pan from the heat.

Pat the pork chops dry with paper towels and season generously with salt and black pepper. In a large ovenproof skillet, warm the remaining 2 tablespoons olive oil over medium-high heat. When the oil shimmers, add the chops and cook until golden brown but not fully done, 4 to 6 minutes per side.

Transfer the skillet to the oven and roast the chops until the internal temperature is around 135°F. It should take about 10 minutes for a pork chop 1 inch thick.

Remove the pork from the oven, quickly add the chopped garlic and the remaining sage leaves to the pan, and baste the pork chops with any rendered fat and oils in the pan.

To serve, slice the pork and spoon some of the juices over the top. Add the potatoes to the cherry peppers, mix together, and spoon everything over the pork. Serve immediately.

A Pork Shoulder Braised with Apples and Onions

The secret to achieving a dish with layers and layers of flavor isn't really that much of a secret at all. Add layers and layers of flavor. Take this recipe as an example. First, start with the pork shoulder, a cheap cut that's well marbled and versatile. In my restaurant I might braise it, cool it, then deglaze it. But at home, I just want to roast pork shoulder and not bother with all those steps. Instead, I add all the ingredients to a Dutch oven, knowing that the braising liquid itself—chicken stock and cider—adds a layer of flavor. The caramelized onions add another. The apples lend a final fall touch. The most important technique is to know when to add the ingredients so they're properly cooked. (Zucchini, for instance, or squash would cook much faster than apples.) That's it. This was my grandmother's style of cooking. Unfussy, simple. It doesn't take a lot of work, but it is delicious.

Serves 4 to 6

SPICE MIXTURE
1 tablespoon allspice berries
1 tablespoon cardamom seeds
   (from about 30 whole pods)
1 tablespoon coriander seeds
1 tablespoon fennel seeds

PORK SHOULDER
4- to 5-pound bone-in pork
   shoulder, tied
Kosher salt and freshly ground
   black pepper

¼ cup plus 3 tablespoons extra-
   virgin olive oil, plus more if
   needed
6 cups chicken stock
2 cups hard cider
6 or 7 sprigs fresh thyme
2 or 3 bay leaves
4 or 5 red torpedo onions or
   small red onions, cut into
   1-inch wedges
3 red apples (about 1 pound),
   halved and cored

Make the spice mixture: With a mortar and pestle or in a small spice grinder, blend together the allspice, cardamom, coriander, and fennel seeds. Set aside.

(recipe continues)

Preheat the oven to 350°F.

Braise the pork: Generously season the pork shoulder all over with salt and pepper.

In a Dutch oven large enough to comfortably fit the pork shoulder and other ingredients, pour in ¼ cup of the olive oil and set over medium heat. Once it is shimmering, add the pork shoulder and sear on all sides, 8 to 10 minutes per side.

Once the pork shoulder has been seared, pour out all but about 1 tablespoon fat. Add the chicken stock and hard cider. The liquid should come halfway up the side of the pork shoulder, so add more liquid if needed. Bring the liquid to a low simmer over medium heat, about 5 minutes.

Add the thyme and bay leaves, cover the Dutch oven, and place in the oven. Cook until the pork is soft and tender, about 3 hours.

Meanwhile, in a large sauté pan, heat the remaining 3 tablespoons oil over medium heat until shimmering. Add the onions and cook until browned and soft, about 5 minutes. Remove the onions from the pan.

Add the apples, flesh-side down, adding more oil if needed. Sear the apples until browned and soft, 5 to 7 minutes.

Once the pork is done, remove the Dutch oven from the oven. Using a small ladle or large spoon, remove and discard any excess fat from the braising liquid. Cover the top of the pork shoulder with the spice mixture, pressing it into the flesh and using some liquid as needed to help it adhere. Add the onions and apples to the braising liquid. Season with salt and pepper to taste.

Return the pot to the oven, uncovered, and continue cooking until the onions and apples are fork-tender, 30 to 45 minutes.

At this point, the pork can be shredded and served immediately with the braised apples and onions.

Or the pork shoulder can be refrigerated uncut until completely cooled and then cut into slices for serving. It can be stored in the refrigerator for up to 1 week. To serve, lay the slices back into a baking dish and pour the braising liquid over the top. Place the dish in the oven at 350°F until warmed through.

Skirt Steak with Shishitos, Hot Cherry Peppers, and Onions

This recipe started as a salad for our babysitter Tenzin, who is a vegetarian. I, clearly, am not. But the flavors of that salad—sweetness, acid, spice, saltiness, and umami—work so well together I knew they would go perfectly with steak. For the record, this combo of hot cherry peppers, shishitos, and red onions, which touches every flavor receptor, works just as well with grilled pork, chicken, or fish. Sometimes I'll add raw cucumbers at the end; sometimes I'll cut the onions into rings and grill them. And if you have leftover steak, just slice it, toss it briefly on the grill, and use.

Serves 4

1¼ pounds skirt steak
6 tablespoons extra-virgin olive oil
2 red onions, cut into 1-inch wedges
Kosher salt
½ pound shishito peppers
Freshly cracked black pepper
1 tablespoon fish sauce
1 tablespoon chili crisp
¼ cup sliced pickled hot cherry peppers
½ cup fresh cilantro leaves
½ cup fresh mint leaves
½ cup fresh parsley leaves
½ cup fresh basil leaves
2 or 3 scallions, sliced
Juice of 1 lime

Allow the steak to come to room temperature.

Warm a large heavy-bottomed sauté pan over medium heat. Add enough oil to coat the bottom of the pan, about 2 tablespoons. Place the onions in the pan, season with salt, and cook until browned and soft, 6 to 7 minutes. Transfer the onions from the pan to a large bowl.

To the same pan, add 1 tablespoon oil and the shishito peppers. Season with salt and cook, turning occasionally, until the shishitos are charred and blistered, 6 to 8 minutes.

(recipe continues)

Transfer the shishitos to the bowl with the onions. Toss the onions and peppers with 1 tablespoon olive oil and salt and black pepper to taste. Add the fish sauce, chili crisp, and pickled peppers. Taste and adjust the amount of chili crisp and pickled peppers based on how much spice you like. Add the fresh cilantro, mint, parsley, and basil and mix.

Dry the skirt steak with paper towels and cut crosswise into pieces that will fit in the same heavy-bottomed sauté pan. Generously season the steak with salt and black pepper.

Heat the pan over medium-high heat. Pour in enough oil to coat the bottom, about 2 tablespoons. When the oil shimmers, add the steak to the pan (in batches, if needed, so as not to overcrowd the pan) and sear for 2 to 3 minutes per side for medium-rare.

Transfer the steak to a cutting board and allow to rest for 5 minutes before slicing against the grain and tossing with the onion/shishito/herb mixture. Spoon any accumulated juices over the steak, top with the scallions and lime juice, and enjoy.

Seared Lamb Loin with Cranberry Beans

Perhaps this recipe should be called Cranberry Beans with Seared Lamb Loin because it really is a showcase for the cranberry bean, aka borlotti bean. What's important to keep in mind is that fresh beans are completely different from dried beans. It's akin to the difference between using fresh herbs and dried herbs. Fresh beans cook up differently than their dried counterparts and yield a firmer texture, too, so if you see fresh shelling beans in the market, buy them. Both are cooked with the same technique, though with a dried bean, since you're basically rehydrating it, the cooking takes longer. I'd even suggest substituting a different fresh bean over using a dried one. Keep testing the beans after 30 minutes; when there's no more crunch, they're done.

About the lamb: As with all meat, please use temperature, rather than time, as a measure of doneness. What might take me 15 minutes to cook might take you 20 or 30. It depends on the oven and on the size of the meat and how much fat that particular animal has. So get a thermometer. It yields a better result than a timer.

Serves 4 to 6

CRANBERRY BEANS
1 pound cranberry beans, 2 cups fresh or 1½ cups dried
1 small carrot, cut into 1-inch pieces
Kosher salt and freshly ground black pepper

FRYING PEPPERS
3 tablespoons extra-virgin olive oil, plus more for drizzling
8 to 12 Jimmy Nardello peppers or other long sweet pepper
Kosher salt

1 celery stalk, thinly sliced
1 small red onion, thinly sliced
3 garlic cloves, sliced
Freshly ground black pepper

LAMB LOIN
1½ to 2 pounds boneless lamb loin with fat attached, at room temperature
Kosher salt and freshly ground black pepper
¼ cup extra-virgin olive oil
10 garlic cloves, peeled but whole
4 or 5 sprigs fresh thyme

(recipe continues)

Cook the cranberry beans: In a medium saucepan, combine the beans with enough water to cover them by 2 inches. Add the carrot, cover the pan, and bring to a slow simmer over medium heat. Do not let the beans boil. Season with 1 tablespoon salt and cook until the beans are soft, about 30 minutes for fresh or about 50 minutes for dried. Season to taste with salt and black pepper. (The beans can be prepared up to a week in advance and kept refrigerated in an airtight container.)

Meanwhile, prepare the frying peppers: In a large sauté pan, heat 3 tablespoons of the olive oil. Add the peppers, season with salt, and cook until they blister and start to soften, about 5 minutes. Add the celery, onion, and garlic, season with salt and black pepper, and cook until the onions are just starting to soften, 5 to 6 minutes. Set aside.

Prepare the lamb loin: Pat the lamb dry and season generously with salt and black pepper. In a large sauté pan, heat the oil over medium heat until shimmering. Add the lamb and cook, turning occasionally, for 10 minutes. Add the garlic and thyme and continue to rotate the lamb loin in the pan until it is browned all over and the internal temperature is between 120° and 135°F for medium-rare to medium, 15 to 20 minutes longer, for a total of 25 to 30 minutes, give or take.

Remove the lamb from the pan and allow to rest on a cutting board for about 5 minutes before slicing.

Drain the cooked cranberry beans and add 4 cups to the frying pepper/onion mixture. Season with salt and black pepper and serve over slices of lamb. Finish the dish with a drizzle of olive oil.

3.

The Hustle

MY FATHER WAS SCRAPPY and enterprising. He owned a barbershop when I was young, and it suited him. Though quiet at home, in social settings he'd transform, holding the floor for a revolving audience. When my brothers and I were small, my mom would dress us in matching outfits, and we'd troop over to the shop so my dad could cut our hair (back then mine was blond and curly, and I had a lot of it). I loved that place. It smelled good, like talcum powder and Barbisol. There was a miniature car for the kiddos to sit in and a stuffed monkey to play with. There was also a room in the back, off-limits to us kids, where my dad took bets, another reason the place suited him. My mom wasn't happy about the gambling, but certain things weren't up to her.

One day my brothers and I came home to the news that my father had sold the barbershop. My parents didn't offer an explanation, and by then we were practiced in the fine art of not asking, so no one talked about it. It took me a few years to realize he'd lost the shop to gambling. To pay the bills, Dad got a job as a corrections

My father with my brother Mike and me, circa 1964

officer at the Union County jail, a boring gig he never enjoyed. Looking back, I can see in my father the same chemical itch my boys and I know so well, the one we need to scratch with novel experiences, travel, new people, and ideas. Where do you go with that when your life is just a few square blocks in Elizabeth?

My father's restless mind would land on new ventures whenever the opportunity presented. Our city had dozens of church festivals and feasts. Name a saint, they had a feast. Ours was the Feast of St. Rocco, which started small, with just a few families selling food in front of their houses on the block, but grew into a bigger thing, with local vendors setting up stalls for the passing crowd. My dad got in on the action. He set up a steak sandwich concession with his sister, my aunt Anita, manning the rented griddles with her husband, John, while she chopped peppers and onions. I got in on it, too, selling cans of soda nearby for fifty cents that I'd bought for a dime a pop. But frying steaks and sausages was hot, pain-in-the-ass work for August, and these feasts could last a week or more. So my grandfather built them a slotted table down in his workshop, and they switched their festival business to a Ping-Pong goldfish toss.

I wish I could say these bursts of industry improved our family's lifestyle, but they didn't. Any extra cash generated went to pay off my father's gambling debts, racked up from his weekly bets on football games. My dad's wins were infrequent but buoying; his losses went unmentioned but were felt, especially by my mother, whose job it was to manage the household budget out of the small stack of cash my father handed her each week, however thin.

When I was around twelve, my father caught a glimpse of the glow necklaces they sold at amusement parks and figured he could make a buck selling them on the boardwalk outside the Miss America pageant in Atlantic City. He bought a bunch in bulk, threw them in the trunk of the car, and roped us and my aunt Theresa (my father's sisters made great wingmen) into coming along. As luck had it, it poured that day, and no one was out on the boardwalk. The venture was a bust. Wet and disgruntled, we all piled back into the car and promptly fell asleep for the drive home. When we woke up, we weren't home at all; he'd driven through the night to Great Adventure amusement park, figuring he'd sell the necklaces there. My mother sat up in alarm, protesting, "You need a permit, Tom! You'll get us arrested!" She had a point, so he headed home. Those necklaces lived in our freezer for years.

It was humiliating, at twelve or thirteen, to walk in the rain peddling something no one wanted. It made me feel bad for my dad, which was itself a crappy feeling. But the person who really caught the short end of my father's schemes was my mother, Beverly. If the world they'd been born into offered little adventure to my dad, it offered even less to her—she played an adjunct role, at best, to the horse she'd hitched herself to. And yet she leaned into being a mom and homemaker with energy and enthusiasm. She somehow found the funds and materials for arts and crafts, for books, for outings. My mom would read my moods and tease out my feelings, which mattered to her. She was endlessly encouraging, and because I trusted her, this shaped my sense of self. I thought of myself as a good artist because she had framed and hung my art on the wall. If she came to every basketball game, it must be because I was worth watching, though how she found the time, I'll never know. She was busy, and I mean *busy*; there were mountains of laundry for my dad and the three of us—the machines were down two flights of stairs in a basement accessed from outside—and each piece got ironed (even the sheets), folded, and put away. Our floors were a daily preoccupation— the linoleum mopped and waxed, carpets vacuumed—and this, more than a conviction about the benefits of fresh air, had her pushing the three of us outdoors at every opportunity. At least twice yearly, she'd tear the whole place apart, pulling everything out of the closets for a deep clean and taking down curtains to be washed. She shopped daily (there was no Costco back then), shlepping home the heavy bags when my grandfather wasn't around to drive her and turning those groceries into a full meal, punctually at 5:30 p.m., for which we were expected to be home.

As you can imagine, she was tired—the three of us didn't even think to lend a hand, nor did my dad—but nonetheless my mom volunteered to chaperone school trips and to lead Cub Scouts. She would make a plate for every wayward cousin and miscreant who trooped through for a comforting hug from "Aunt Bev." How she pulled it all off is a mystery to me, though it probably helped that there was a robust cohort of family and close friends doing the same thing, while dishing drama to keep everyone entertained (my mom could gossip with the best of them). I've got a snapshot somewhere of my mom at age thirty or so, on a class trip, slim, in a red, white, and blue poncho, with her 1970s hair flip and an easy smile. Every kid thinks their mom is pretty and special; mine really was. This is the image I hold in my mind when I think of her even now, at eighty-five.

My mother's great aspiration was to get out of Elizabeth and own her own home. My father's sisters gave her a hard time for it (that classic Italian reproach, "You think you're too good for us?"). But it was for me and my brothers, not herself, that she wanted more, and she never stopped trying. Even after the nuns had written me off, my mother sent away hopefully for an application to Pingry, a prep school in tony Basking Ridge that had once been in Elizabeth. She filled out the application, and I was accepted. My father was against the idea, worried about paying for it, no doubt. Still, my mom might have been able to make it happen—Grandpa Mike had been frugal and would have helped from his savings—if I hadn't also resisted, pushing back about leaving my friends. Against me and my father, my mom didn't stand a chance, nor was she raised to assert herself. I was starting to get into trouble at this point, messing around in the streets. Today, as a parent, I can only imagine how that must have scared her, how powerless to improve my lot she must have felt.

It's complicated, looking back at my parents this way, seeing their limitations alongside their strengths. My father's appetite for risk could be dangerous or heroic, depending on who was telling the story. My father once ran into a burning building to save people and it made the papers. He had a code of honor that was consistent with his time and place. Out at a diner with my mom one night, some local wise guy and his pals were loudly tossing off obscenities in the next booth. My father turned and asked him nicely to keep it down in earshot of my mother. He didn't, so my father asked again. The third time, my dad pulled out his service pistol from the jail and put it in the wise guy's face. He stopped.

Stories like these burnished my father's legend in my mind, and there were other things about him that made me proud, like his shiny Cadillac (my friends' fathers drove Fords). But as I got older, my grasp of the situation changed and the feelings curdled. Their dads might be driving Fords, but those friends had their own rooms, some of them even in houses, while my brothers and I shared a single room in a crappy two-bedroom apartment. When my mom urged us to be quiet so Dad could sleep in after a night shift, I knew the extra work was to pay off his gambling debts, not to get us into a better neighborhood or make my mom's life easier. How many of us men have these memories of our fathers twisted up so tightly between deep love and contempt?

Like I said, it's complicated. It's true that my father seemed to choose gambling over us. But it's also true that he came home when I was about fifteen and handed me a brochure for the Culinary Institute of America (CIA), saying, "Hey, Tommy, you should check this out." There he was again, thinking about me on his own time. By this point, I pretty much knew college wasn't going to be in the cards for me, but cooking school was something different. I was intrigued. The brochure said applicants needed to work at two restaurants before they were eligible to apply. I didn't think the snack shack counted, so if I wanted to go to the CIA, I'd need professional experience. With the exception of Spirito's, though, what did we know from restaurants? We ate at home. But once again, my dad could help. He was well liked, and he knew people. He reached out to his friend Phil Gurcia, who installed HVAC systems in restaurants, and he got me an interview at a real one, a place called Evelyn's.

The original Evelyn's opened in the 1930s in Belmar, New Jersey, thirty-five miles south of us, and was legendary for its fried shrimp, crab, scrod, lobster . . . you name it. My interview was at their second location, in Elizabeth. Unlike at a lot of other seafood places, the fish at Evelyn's was fresh and much of it was local. It wasn't a gourmet place, but they cared about quality.

I didn't think they'd hire me because I was only fifteen, but they did, as a weekend busboy. Talk about hustling. The work was mind-numbing, just as you'd expect from a seafood restaurant that did a thousand covers a night, a blur of wiping, stacking, and shlepping, but the frenetic pace acted on my chaos brain in the same way working all the stations at the Gran Centurions had: It cleared my vision and made me sure of what to do next. And as I'd ferry plates into the dish pit in the kitchen, I'd steal glances at the cooks, working the dinner rush with a purpose and intensity I could feel. Even if I didn't exactly know what each of them was doing, I decided I wanted to do it, too. Fat chance of that, though. The men on the line were pros, full-timers, and I was still in high school, with baseball and basketball practices after school. The only weekend job on offer was the one they'd given me, staggering under stacks of dirty plates.

The summer after graduation, I got my chance. I picked up full-time hours and they moved me into the kitchen, where I quickly learned about hierarchy. All the action at Evelyn's was centered close to the heat. During service, the chef and line cooks were dropping fish into the fryer or popping fillets onto metal plates and under the broiler, then sautéing them for a second on pickup. Behind them, and a clear rung down the ladder, stood two breaders, whose entire job consisted of dredging the fish in a mixture of bread crumbs and flour. Behind

High school graduation, 1980

them, as far from the heat as you could be and still be on the line, was the bench, my station. My job was to open clams and oysters and trim the fillets. Menial work certainly, but I was in the kitchen at last, and thrilled to be in the mix.

The Evelyn's crew was older; some were in college, plus one or two single mothers trying to make ends meet. To me, they seemed worldly and glamorous. I had hair back then, I was in good shape, and I had girls telling me they liked my eyes, so I didn't lack for confidence. The waitresses didn't seem overly concerned about my age as they invited me out to parties or post-shift drinks. It was intoxicating, literally and figuratively.

Though the front of house was mostly women—in a *New York Times* review from 1975, writer Jean Hewitt singled them out as being "smartly dressed in shirts and ties and trim black jumpers"—the kitchen crew was a rough and ragtag bunch of addicts, weirdos, and misfits. Bobby Connolly, a tall, muscular, sandy-haired guy, was the de facto leader. He was the sous, not the chef—that was a guy named Alfred—but Bobby ran the kitchen during service and he set the tone. What a tone. Bobby was a lifer, one of those guys who was drawn to the kitchen, not as a vocation, but because there was probably nowhere else he could spend his working hours fucked up, in charge, and, despite this, actually good at the job. There was something dangerous and seductive about Bobby, an alpha energy that everyone in that kitchen felt.

Bobby took a shine to me. By now I too was a committed partyer, casually (and stupidly) smoking or tossing back anything someone handed me. Looking back, I can see how risky this was, but back then, seeing an authority like Bobby high and crushing it felt like permission. I believed I was a better version of myself when I was high, talkative, and open. Weed quickly became an important social unguent, a crutch. I smoked so much, in fact, that I started to deal small amounts to subsidize my habit.

But while I admired Bobby's command of the kitchen, Bobby wasn't how I wanted to end up. Outside of work, he was a mess. As the novelty wore off, I could see the difference between us: Bobby had a job to do, and it was cooking; it's how he paid his bills. But I was hooked on the cooking itself, and I realized I wanted more than just a paycheck from it. In my spare time, I started buying chickens so I could practice breaking them down in under a minute. At home I'd practice on ingredients I'd always known, but I started playing around with flavors that were new to me, like turning my grandfather's mussels and clams into a Provençal stew. I'd always loved to read, and, along with a few magazine subscriptions my mother had bought me, I was growing my library of classic cookbooks with titles like *Great*

Chefs of France, which I read like a novel. Celebrated French chefs were now on my radar, like Alain Chapel, Michel Guérard, and the Troisgros brothers, along with up-and-comers like Alice Waters and Jeremiah Tower, avatars of California cuisine, who were carving out a new vernacular for American food. All of them put names and faces to a new thought: I could be a chef, someone who was dedicated to technique, as Pépin was, and not just a cook.

All that reading didn't translate into skills, though. My first week on the bench, I tanked. I misread orders as they came out. I pulled the wrong fish for the order. I couldn't keep up. Though I was popular with the guys, my mistakes seriously hobbled the kitchen. It was humbling, and a good first lesson on how every single position in a kitchen, from the lowest to the highest, is necessary and impactful. Much to my embarrassment, after only a few days I got transferred down to the prep kitchen.

Away from the hot line and the rigors of service, the prep kitchen was a different beast altogether. Without tickets coming in, the pressure came not from timing but from the sheer volume of work to do. There were king crab shells to slice open, fish to debone, and mountains of shrimp to peel. The first day I was led to a 150-pound tubful and set to the fiddly and tedious work. When it was done, they gave me another. Hours later, one of the waitresses nudged me awake; I had fallen asleep standing up. As I emerged blearily from the prep kitchen, I caught Bobby and the others laughing their asses off. That was my first taste of kitchen hazing.

The man who ran the prep kitchen was also about as far from Bobby as humanly possible. He was an older Black man named Slim, who hailed from South Carolina. Slim was in charge of all the actual cooking that went on at Evelyn's, by which I mean he made everything that required attention and judgment, like stocks, sauces, and vegetables. Slim took me under his wing. He didn't talk much, which was fine (I was used to men like that). He taught by working alongside me. Now and then he'd say, "They give me recipes but I don't use them." The idea of Slim needing a recipe was laughable. He cooked purely by experience and intuition. To this day, I think of him as the first real chef I ever met, a world apart from the famous ones I'd been reading about in my culinary magazines, but cut from the same cloth.

After a few months with Slim, I made my way back to the hot line, cocky and unbowed. By this time I was telling anyone who would listen that I planned to be a chef. No one laughed or dismissed the idea. Green as I was, they could see that I was serious about cooking, much more than they were.

There was one woman on the breading station, I think her name was Jill, who kept herself slightly apart from the partying herd. She had always seemed interested in me and my ambition. On a rare slow day, while I was messing around at my station, Jill walked over to me and said, "So you want to be a chef? Make me something." Though being put on the spot in school had made me freeze up, here, amazingly, an idea immediately appeared. I had recently read about a sauce called beurre blanc, an emulsion of butter and wine. Beurre blanc is simple but temperamental: Heat it too hard and it'll break; too gently and it won't cohere. I'd never made it before, but here I was, with time and tubs of butter at my disposal and an audience, so why not try? I heated up some wine and shallots until they softened and grew fragrant, then threw in a splash of white vinegar and let it reduce. When the liquid was nearly gone, I whisked in cubes of butter. I had read that the sauce took seasoning well, so I added a fistful of the freeze-dried chives we kept on hand for the fried calamari, then gently warmed some crabmeat in the sauce. Next I quickly pan-fried a fillet of fluke and slid it onto a plate, with the crabmeat on top and the remaining beurre blanc drizzled over it. I presented the dish to my very first diner.

Jill's eyes lit up as she chewed. "Tom," she said, "this is *very* good." Forty-plus years later, the expression on her face at that moment is still vivid in my mind. It was the first time this hustle of mine elicited a spark of genuine delight in someone outside of my family, a relative stranger, which made it all the more validating. That may have marked a turning point, a point at which I understood that I could really pull this thing off—not just for the paycheck or the job security—and that it would ignite pleasure, excitement, and approval in others. This, then, was how I would find my way back to the real me.

4

Freaks and Leeks

NOW THAT I WAS AT EVELYN'S full-time, I had some money in my pocket and my partying took on a new dimension, with later nights and harder drugs. That didn't sit well with my father, and we clashed. Life at home was more cramped than ever with three man-sized boys still crammed into one bedroom. It wasn't pretty.

I also had a serious girlfriend, a brainy and beautiful brunette (that's my type) named Regi Slavinski, who was studying at Montclair State. We'd been together since we were fifteen, sometimes tumultuously, but we were in love. Not only was Regi driven and smart, she was good-hearted and knew how to have fun. Regi wanted to get away from her old man, too, so we found ourselves a cheap apartment in a big Tudor building in East Orange known as the White Castle, named not for its stonework but for its residents, who were mainly faculty at nearby Upsala College and stood out in the largely Black neighborhood. On a windy autumn morning, I drove my stuff over to the new place: clothes, albums, cookbooks. A boyhood in boxes. I'm sure Regi's parents didn't like us moving in together any more than mine did, but for an eighteen-year-old I was making good money and could swing the rent, so what could they do?

By now I had worked all the stations at Evelyn's, moving from the bench to the salad station and on to the bakery, where the ancient oven racks would sag from the heat and crush the cheesecakes I had so carefully rotated. I had manned the fryer and the broiler and was trusted enough to take the company truck down to the flagship in Belmar to pick up fish. There was no longer a new station to aspire to, and I itched to try something new.

The CIA was still in the back of my mind, but now I had rent to pay and wasn't ready to give up my income or move away from Regi to Dutchess County, so instead I tried to give myself a culinary education at home, working my way systematically through the cookbooks in my collection, like I had with Jacques Pépin's. I started with Elizabeth David's 1960 masterpiece, *French Provincial Cooking*, which refreshingly assumed that its readers could already cook. (Rather than measurements, the recipes called for "some" of this and "a bit" of that.)

I made coq au vin, duck pâtés, and homemade saucisses de Campagne, which weren't much different from the Italian pork sausage I'd eaten growing up, except for the spices. I cooked through Pépin's *La Methode* (of course), Alice Waters's *Chez Panisse Menu Cookbook*, and Michel Guérard's *Cuisine Gourmande*. I taught myself to make fresh pasta and puff pastry, turning out dozens of iterations until I'd gotten the shapes down. I'd scrutinize the results against

the pictures in the books, wondering if I'd gotten it right. With zero fine-dining experience of my own and no one to teach me, I wasn't sure. What was clear was that I needed a change of scenery so I could keep learning.

I left Evelyn's and landed at a busy red sauce joint in Union, New Jersey, called the Chestnut Tavern, which was like a slightly more worldly cousin of Spirito's. I was younger than the cook I'd replaced by a couple of decades, and Evelyn's had taught me to work fast, so I was buzzing through my prep in an hour. This gave me time to help Stan, the guy who ran lunch and was in charge of butchering. From him I learned how to break down a massive leg of veal into its component parts—rump roast, top round, and cutlets, which we'd feed through a wall-mounted tenderizer for marsala, piccata, or scallopini. There wasn't a lot happening culinarily at the Chestnut Tavern, though, and it didn't take long before the itch returned. The owner's son Richard suggested I might want some hotel experience, and to my untrained ears that sounded interesting and fancy. He made a call, and I got hired as a line cook at the Hilton in Secaucus.

The Hilton had a fine-dining room and a smaller café/coffee shop, but its main business was conventions and banquets. We all had our respective roles, but everyone jumped in for the banquets because they were enormous and demanded all hands on deck. Dinner for a few hundred was the norm, and frequently we were serving two or three parties at once. Brunch might be attended by five hundred conventioneers.

Working at the Hilton was an education in cooking at scale. There was no time to sweat the small stuff. Scrambled eggs for five hundred? You dump forty flats of eggs (each flat is two dozen) whole into a revolving stand mixer, then strain out the shells. Hollandaise was achieved by whipping ten dozen egg yolks in the same machine, setting a bunch of lit Sternos underneath, then tossing in some clarified butter. *Voilà!* There's your two hundred eggs Benedict. We'd finish batches of a hundred plates at a time, top them with flat cloches, and stack them inside a Queen Mary—a giant warming cabinet on wheels—that would be rolled to the edge of the dining room. From there, dozens of waiters would slide out the plates and ferry them to tables, like a march of penguins, and by the time they returned, the next Queen Mary was full and ready to unload. The pace was relentless. I remember pausing only occasionally, like when a rabbi would show up to prep the place for kosher events. He'd blowtorch our workspace and say a quick blessing while we all stood by respectfully. There was a system for everything, and efficiency was king.

More care was taken with the food in the hotel's restaurant. My boss was Steve Sharrod, a nice enough guy in his thirties with a comically thick Boston accent. We served what you'd expect from a menu of Continental hits, circa 1983: chicken cordon bleu, beef Wellington, veal Oscar, chocolate mousse. Within a week Steve took me off the line and promoted me to overseeing dinner service. This was exciting; the job included coming up with nightly specials and then figuring out how to break them down into executable parts that could be delegated to the line. For ideas, I went straight to my books and magazines. I was determined to offer something resembling the lighter, ingredient-driven dishes I was reading about at Chez Panisse, at Ken Frank's La Toque in West Hollywood, at Jonathan Waxman's Michael's in Santa Monica.

For a time, it worked. For one thing, I was getting an education in managing people and running large events—one of the reasons I'm not intimidated when I'm asked to cater huge parties today. I liked the folks I met there—a ribald Filipino named Junior with a ton of experience on cruise ships who kept us in stitches, and Pat Minnick, the easygoing and diligent dining room manager. Pat's wife had just had a baby, and given all the chaos a baby brings, they were looking for a new home for their puppy, Sammy. Naturally, I adopted her, thus starting my lifelong devotion to happy, clever black dogs. I came up with specials like seared scallops with raspberry vinaigrette, or salmon with Chinese mustard and braised leeks. Hardly groundbreaking, but the guests seemed to like them.

I could have stayed at the Hilton and done well. The pay was good, I was almost a boss, and I was getting praised for my specials. But something was off, and I knew it. I sensed (even if no one else seemed to) that I shouldn't be in charge. I wasn't learning. I was rolling out dishes based on the reading I'd done, and while they seemed okay, they lacked something, though I couldn't have told you yet what it was. The itch came back, only now I understood it better. I needed to go somewhere I could grow.

One day, I saw an advertisement in a local Jersey paper for a sous-chef position at a new restaurant in Millburn called 40 Main Street, which described itself as serving "New American cuisine." My go-to book for cribbing specials at this point was *Cooking the Nouvelle Cuisine in America* by David Liederman. Nouvelle cuisine, which had taken France by storm in the 1970s, was all about lightening and expanding the French palate; Paul Bocuse had gone to Asia and brought back its flavors, and Michel Guérard was swapping out heavy béchamels and veloutés for simpler reductions and sauces made with novel ingredients, like kiwifruit. Nouvelle cuisine also shook up the notion of fine service. Rather than serving tableside in the old formal manner, chefs would prepare dishes individually in the kitchen, allowing their personal style to appear on the plate. New American cuisine took all of this a step further by marrying these new techniques to an American melting-pot sensibility. I immediately called the number in the ad.

I was a day too late. Danny Cannizzo, the owner of 40 Main Street, had already hired a sous-chef, but he offered me a line cook position instead. I took a look around: There was a spit and polish to the place; care had gone into it. The kitchen wasn't big, but it was brand new and well appointed. The dining room was filled with art, paintings mostly made by Danny's wife, Barbara, plus quilts and prints. The chef was Jim Smith, a CIA graduate from Madison, Wisconsin, and his menu was seasonal and ambitious: cold duck galantine, scallop ceviche, pheasant roulade, sweetbreads with morels, veal tournedos with wild mushrooms, veal with blueberry sauce. Line cook was a step down from the job I held at the Secaucus Hilton, but everything else about the place was two or three steps up. I took the job.

40 Main was ahead of its time in the sense that nearly every day we concocted the menu anew, and Jim insisted on the highest-quality

sourcing possible, directly from farmers when we could. Whereas my previous jobs were about speed and volume, here we were making dishes whose complexity demanded time and genuine skill. To make that galantine, we'd bone the whole bird painstakingly from the back, layer on a chilled forcemeat of sieved meat and seasonings, roll the whole thing up, and tie it off to be poached or roasted. Efficiency still mattered, but technique and freshness won the day.

While the food was better and more exciting than any I'd cooked before, in those first couple of weeks, one thing became clear: The tiny kitchen, like all the kitchens I'd known, was filled with bona fide freaks. Jim, a wiry little guy in his early thirties, would start service by calling out, "Time to get right!," which meant popping out back to get stoned before the first order came in. An aside: It's important to remember here that kitchens then were run by a generation of people who'd come up in the 1960s and '70s, for whom smoking a joint at work was what drinking a cup of coffee is today. But even by the relaxed standards of the day, Jim was next level—he'd get so high I was surprised his feet touched the floor, yet he could still juggle twenty entrées at once, like a concert master. The kitchen was permanently sweltering, so much so that Jim would strip to a T-shirt and jock strap, tie on two aprons—one in the front, the other in the back—and cook pretty much nude from the waist down.

There was a talented young woman named Kate Formacella on garde-manger who had the misfortune of also being gorgeous, and Jim hit on her relentlessly. Today we know that's harassment, but back then it was an unremarkable condition of employment, just one more thing women were expected to tolerate if they wanted in on the action. The second garde-manger, a fleshy mountain of a guy named Rondo Resnick, had an ongoing feud with another guy on the line, a nose-down cook named Tom Carlin, and the two would chase each other around the kitchen, threatening violence. All the bussers belonged to the same Persian family—Jimmy El Sawi and his cousins, Waffa and Walla—but the Iran hostage crisis was still fresh in the country's mind, so they called themselves Egyptian. The waitress, Herta, was a large fräulein who flirted with everyone

Dan Cannizzo, me, and Jerry Bryan

in a thick German accent and walked with a heavy limp. As if the space weren't tight enough, Danny would frequently drop in (when he wasn't singing opera to the guests), as would his mother, Mama Rose, and his brother, a large man with such a knack for knocking everything over we nicknamed him Crash.

There was one exception to the circus: Jerry Bryan, the guy who'd beaten me to the sous-chef job by a day. Jerry was the adult in the room. Clean-cut and rail thin, with piercing blue eyes and an upright military bearing, he had been a pathfinder in the 82nd Airborne before he became a chef. Jerry held the place together, and he was pretty much my opposite in every way; he was Southern and disciplined and had a New York City résumé—he'd worked under the great Leslie Revsin at Restaurant Leslie in Greenwich Village. Jerry didn't smoke and barely drank. He was married and owned a house, which he returned to at night while the rest of us headed out to party. He was demanding but fair, a by-the-book guy whose ethos reminded me of my grandfather's, which may have been why I liked him from the start.

Jerry was my direct superior, and he could have been a dick about it, but he wasn't. We quickly established ourselves as partners and collaborators. A typical day had us getting in around noon to sit down with Jim and kick around ideas for the dinner menu. On the line, Jerry and I worked in that easy, loose way of matched equals, challenging each other and ourselves. We built a rhythm, and soon we were in lockstep and on fire, enough so that Jim stopped coming in at night, leaving it to us. That's when Jerry and I really bonded, and we became close friends as well as coworkers. Eventually Jim handed us the pre-shift meetings, too, which meant we could take our ideas and run with them. Jerry and I were ambitious: We didn't want 40 Main to be just a great restaurant in Millburn, we wanted it to be a great restaurant, period. And so we pushed Rondo and Tom to execute at increasingly elite levels and the servers to hustle faster, calling out "Hands!" from the pass. Herta would grouse as she lumbered over, saying, "Jah, jah, I am comink."

Our work did not go unnoticed. In August 1984, we got a three-star review from *New York Times* restaurant critic Anne Semmes, who wrote that the food was "thoughtfully planned and carefully executed" with "Nouvelle American overtones. . . . With such appealing food, and in such charming surroundings (especially if the owner can be persuaded to sing a couple of arias), an evening at 40 Main Street can be theater itself."

It felt great to be noticed. My mother clipped all the reviews, and even my father seemed proud; we threw him a fiftieth birthday party at the restaurant and my parents invited a swarm of cousins and friends. But in the back of my mind, I knew I hadn't yet arrived. The itch came back, only this time it was for more than work. I was reading my way through Regi's books from college and found myself growing interested in the larger world. The early '80s were an incredible time for music and art in New York City, and in my free hours I'd head there to visit museums and galleries and hear live bands. Ideas beget ideas. Imagination feeds imagination. The work at 40 Main Street was pushing me forward creatively, and I found myself seeking out creativity wherever I could find it. Modern art electrified me. Literature and architecture were exciting. Looking back, I can see how hungry I was for education in many spheres, not just food.

So it should come as no surprise that after about a year at 40 Main Street, I gave my notice. A job in New York City was the obvious next step, but I was nervous. I had no idea if I had what it took, but I knew I had good knife skills and was a hard, fast worker, so surely somebody could be persuaded to hire me. Jerry encouraged me to go for it. And 40 Main Street gave me the confidence to try.

Winter
Recipes

My Grandpa's Beet Salad

My grandmother liked to cook. Especially when she was on a manic high. She'd bake and bake and bake until every table of my grandparents' house was covered in pies and plates of cookies. When she was depressed, however, she hardly got out of bed. My grandfather had to take over. One of his specialties, which he made every Christmas, was this beet salad. I don't know where it came from. I never asked and I've never seen anything like this in any Italian cookbook. But it was one of the highlights of our Christmas meal, where it was the perfect complement to the omnipresent salt cod. The earthiness of the beets is paired with the umami-bombs of anchovies, a bunch of herbs, and the saltiness of the olives. My grandfather made this on Christmas Eve and let it sit overnight, so all the flavors commingled, and I recommend you do the same.

Serves 8 to 10

2½ pounds medium beets (10 to 12), stems removed

Kosher salt

1 medium fennel bulb, halved, cored, and thinly sliced

1 medium red onion, halved and thinly sliced

One 10.5-ounce jar artichoke hearts in olive oil, drained and chopped

1 cup oil-cured black olives, pitted

1 cup drained giardiniera (from a 12-ounce jar)

2 celery stalks, finely chopped

5 small garlic cloves, chopped

One 2-ounce tin anchovy fillets, chopped

1 bunch parsley, leaves picked and roughly chopped

½ cup extra-virgin olive oil

Coarsely ground black pepper

2 tablespoons red wine vinegar, plus more to taste

Add the beets to a large pot of cold water. Season with salt. Place over medium heat and cook until soft, 1 hour to 1 hour 30 minutes. The water should stay at a low simmer but never come to a boil. You'll know the beets are cooked when they offer no resistance when poked with a knife or metal skewer.

(recipe continues)

Meanwhile, in a large bowl, combine the fennel, onion, artichokes, olives, giardiniera, celery, garlic, anchovies, and parsley. Add ¼ cup of the olive oil. Season with black pepper. Season with salt (taste it; because of the anchovy you don't have to be as generous with the salt).

Once the beets are cooked through, run them under cold water. The skins will slip off; discard the skins. When the beets are cool enough to handle, slice into wedges roughly ½ to ¾ inch thick. Place the beets in a bowl and add the remaining ¼ cup olive oil and the vinegar. Season with salt.

Mix the seasoned beets into the bowl with the salad ingredients. Before serving, taste for acidity. Add more vinegar and salt if needed.

The beets can be served right away, but letting the salad sit for at least a few hours, or ideally overnight, will allow the flavors to combine. If refrigerating overnight, bring back to cool room temperature before serving.

Delicious Ancient Vegetables, aka Jerusalem Artichokes

The first time I saw Jerusalem artichokes used in a dish, I was eating at Marc Veyrat's three-star restaurant l'Auberge de l'Eridan in Haute-Savoie. He called the dish Steamed Ancient Vegetables. It consisted of truffles, leeks, and Jerusalem artichokes. It was simple, earthy, and completely delicious. After that, I searched for Jerusalem artichokes every time I visited the farmers' market. For a long time I was frustrated in my search, but gradually they began to appear. (Jerusalem artichokes grow well in the New York tri-state area.) As an ingredient, they are one of my favorites. They are versatile and shine in many ways, whether roasted, thinly sliced and pickled with mustard seed, or made into a soup. Here they are the centerpiece of a warm salad.

Serves 4 as a side

- 2 tablespoons extra-virgin olive oil
- 4 ounces slab bacon, roughly chopped
- 1 small red onion, roughly chopped
- 1 leek, white part only, roughly chopped
- 1½ pounds Jerusalem artichokes, scrubbed and sliced into rough ½-inch pieces
- Kosher salt
- 7 sprigs fresh thyme, plus more (optional) for serving
- 2 garlic cloves, sliced
- 8 ounces cremini mushrooms, roughly sliced
- ¼ cup chicken stock
- ½ lemon, sliced into half-moons
- ¾ cup chestnuts, roasted and peeled
- Freshly ground black pepper
- Chopped fresh parsley (optional), for serving

Preheat the oven to 400°F.

In a Dutch oven with a tight-fitting lid, warm the olive oil over medium-low heat until shimmering. Add the bacon and cook for 2 to 3 minutes to render the fat. Add the onion and leek and stir to coat.

(recipe continues)

Add the Jerusalem artichokes and cook everything together, stirring often, until the onions and leeks are soft and translucent and the Jerusalem artichokes are starting to soften, 7 to 10 minutes. Season with salt and add the sprigs of thyme and garlic. Stir together and continue cooking for 2 to 3 minutes.

Add the mushrooms and chicken stock and season with salt. Mix together and cook, stirring occasionally, until the mushrooms soften slightly, about 5 minutes. Add the lemon slices and chestnuts and season with salt and pepper.

Cover the Dutch oven and transfer to the oven. Bake until all the veggies are soft and tender, 35 to 40 minutes.

Top the vegetables with some additional thyme or chopped parsley, season with salt and pepper, and serve immediately.

Very Chunky Cranberry Sauce

Like every other kid in the 1970s, I grew up eating canned cranberry sauce once a year on Thanksgiving. It wasn't until I got into professional kitchens in my twenties that I even realized cranberries could—and should—be treated as a worthwhile ingredient. This zesty sauce, which maintains the texture of the cranberries, is now my contribution to the Thanksgiving meal, which we have every year with my in-laws. Of course, the canned stuff is still there—my father-in-law's wife, Andrea, prefers it—but at least my kids will grow up knowing cranberries don't always come out of a can.

Makes 1¾ cups

1 large orange
One 12-ounce package fresh
   cranberries

½ cup sugar
1 tablespoon minced fresh ginger

Use a vegetable peeler to remove the zest of the orange in strips (leaving behind the bitter white pith). Stack the strips together and thinly slice to create matchstick-size pieces. Juice the orange and set aside.

Add the orange zest to a small pot of cold water. Bring to a boil and cook for about 10 seconds. Drain the water and repeat the process two more times. Drain well.

In a medium pot, combine the cranberries, orange juice, sugar, ginger, and orange zest (reserve about 1 tablespoon zest for serving, if desired). Bring to a boil over high heat. Reduce the heat to low and simmer, stirring occasionally, until the cranberries burst and the sauce thickens slightly, 15 to 20 minutes.

Remove from the heat, transfer to a serving bowl, and serve either warm or cold. Garnish with orange zest if desired.

Storage: This cranberry sauce can be made in advance and kept refrigerated for 3 to 5 days or frozen for 3 months.

My Thanksgiving Stuffing

This stuffing is all thanks to Amy Scherber, the founder of Amy's Bread in New York City. I met Amy when she worked at Mondrian. At the time she was dating my friend the chef Kerry Heffernan. She was always interested in baking and decided to do a *stage* in bakeries around the city. When she returned, I asked her what she wanted to do. She said she was thinking of leaving to work at Tom Cat, probably one of the best bakeries in the city at the time. "Why don't you bake right here at this restaurant?" I asked her. "I don't know if I can," she said, unsure if her bread was up to snuff. We made a deal. I said she could start baking bread at Mondrian and I'd start paying once I thought we could serve it. Within a week, I was paying her. She proved to be a master of the loaf, and the reason why we had the most amazing bread basket in the city.

Soon we were selling breads on the weekends. As folks headed out to the Hamptons, they'd stop by to pick up their bread from Amy. Shortly thereafter she opened Amy's Bread, and the rest is history. Among one of her early triumphs was her raisin fennel bread, which I loved then and love now. It's the perfect combination of sweet and savory for Thanksgiving stuffing. If you can't find a raisin fennel bread, this recipe uses a regular Pullman loaf but replicates the flavors with added fennel seed and golden raisins.

Makes one 9 × 13-inch dish/serves 10 to 12

Softened butter for the gratin dish

2 pounds breakfast sausage links

1 large fennel bulb, finely chopped

1 large carrot, finely chopped

2 celery stalks, finely chopped

1 large leek, white part only, finely chopped

1 medium onion, finely chopped

2 garlic cloves, finely chopped

Kosher salt and freshly ground black pepper

1 cup golden raisins

8 tablespoons unsalted butter, melted

One 2-pound loaf Pullman bread, cut into 1-inch cubes (see Note)

6 sprigs fresh thyme, leaves picked

(ingredients continue on next page)

8 fresh sage leaves, chopped

2 tablespoons fennel seeds

1 cup freshly grated Parmesan cheese

6 large eggs, whisked

3 cups chicken stock, or as needed

Preheat the oven to 350°F. Butter a 9 × 13-inch gratin dish.

In a large sauté pan, cook the sausage over medium heat, turning occasionally, until browned, 10 to 12 minutes. Remove the pan from the heat. Transfer the sausage to a cutting board, leaving the rendered fat in the pan. Cut the sausage into ¼-inch pieces and set aside.

Return the sauté pan to medium heat. Add the chopped fennel, carrot, celery, leek, onion, and garlic. Season with salt and pepper. Cook, stirring often, until the vegetables have softened, about 10 minutes.

In a large bowl, combine the sausage, sautéed vegetables, raisins, melted butter, bread cubes, thyme leaves, sage, fennel seeds, and Parmesan. Thoroughly mix in the eggs. Slowly add chicken stock just until the mixture is moist. Season with salt and pepper and mix together.

Loosely pack the stuffing into the buttered gratin dish. Cover with foil and bake for 30 minutes. Uncover and bake until browned, another 20 to 30 minutes. Serve immediately.

Storage: The stuffing keeps covered and refrigerated for up to 1 week.

Note: I like to cut the bread into cubes when it's fresh because it's easier to cut that way. Then I let it sit out, uncovered, for a day or two to dry it out.

Very Quick Chicken Soup (×3)

With two young kids at home, colds and flu are the gifts that keep on giving. That's when I make this soup, which keeps in the fridge for the entire week. You can make it in a stockpot, sure, but if you have a pressure cooker, this deeply flavorful soup comes together in just 20 minutes. (A pressure cooker can reach temperatures of 375° to 400°F, whereas if you're cooking this in water, the hottest it'll ever get is 212°F.) Lori prefers it without the pasta (carbs!), but if she's not around, I go for the classic chicken noodle version. Either way, it's comfort food at its finest.

Serves 6 to 8

1 whole chicken (4 to 5 pounds)
4 sprigs fresh parsley
4 sprigs fresh thyme
2 carrots, cut into 1- to 2-inch pieces
2 parsnips, peeled and cut into 1- to 2-inch pieces
2 celery stalks, cut into 1- to 2-inch pieces

2 leeks, white parts only, sliced into rings
1 large onion, peeled and halved
Kosher salt and freshly ground black pepper
1 pound pasta, any shape (optional; I like small shapes, such as ditalini)
Freshly grated Parmesan cheese (optional), for serving

PRESSURE COOKER METHOD

Place the whole chicken and the parsley and thyme sprigs in a pressure cooker, cover with water, and cook on high pressure for 20 minutes. Let the steam release naturally. Remove the chicken from the pressure cooker and shred it when cool enough to handle; set aside on a plate.

Add the carrots, parsnips, celery, leeks, and onion to the pressure cooker. Seal again and cook on high pressure for an additional 4 minutes. Let the steam release naturally.

(recipe continues)

Remove the onion halves and discard. Return the chicken to the soup with the vegetables. Season generously with salt and pepper and serve with Parmesan, if using.

STOVETOP METHOD

Cut the chicken into quarters.

In a stockpot or large soup pot, combine the chicken and 16 cups water. Add the parsley and thyme sprigs. Bring to a simmer over medium heat. Season with salt. Reduce the heat to low and simmer gently, skimming the top regularly to remove the solids that float up, until the broth is fragrant, about 30 minutes.

Add the carrots, parsnips, celery, leeks, and onion and continue to simmer until the chicken is cooked and the vegetables are tender, another 20 minutes. Generously season with salt and pepper.

Remove the chicken with a slotted spoon and transfer to a plate. Remove the onion halves and discard. Once it is cool enough to handle, shred the chicken and return it to the pot with the vegetables. Season with more salt and pepper if desired and serve with Parmesan, if using.

INSTRUCTIONS FOR WHEN LORI ISN'T HOME

While the chicken is cooking, bring a large pot of salted water to a boil over high heat. Add the pasta and cook until al dente according to the package directions.

Remove the chicken with a slotted spoon and shred it. Return it to the pot with the vegetables. Add the cooked pasta to the soup. Ladle the soup into bowls and season with more salt and pepper and Parmesan as desired.

Storage: If storing leftovers, store the soup separate from the pasta. Leftovers will keep for 3 to 5 days in the refrigerator or for up to 3 months in the freezer.

————

Happy Wife, Happy Life Soup

A version of caldo verde, a Portuguese soup with kale, clams, chorizo, and chickpeas, this is a favorite of my wife, Lori, that I cook for her when I owe her an apology. But this is a good soup, even when I'm not in the doghouse, for whenever you want a nourishing meal that keeps for a long time and comes together quickly.

Serves 4 to 6

3 tablespoons extra-virgin olive oil
1 small red onion, sliced
1 small fennel bulb, roughly chopped
6 ounces Spanish chorizo, roughly chopped
1 leek, white part only, sliced
8 garlic cloves, 3 sliced and 5 peeled and halved
2 heads lacinato kale, stemmed and midribs removed, leaves roughly chopped

1 cup white wine
1 cup chopped fresh parsley
24 small to medium clams, scrubbed and purged
1 quart chicken stock (plus more if you want extra liquid)
Kosher salt and freshly ground black pepper
One 16-ounce can chickpeas, drained and rinsed

In a large soup pot or Dutch oven, heat the olive oil over medium heat until shimmering. Slowly add the onion and fennel and cook until lightly browned, about 5 minutes. Add the chorizo, leek, and sliced garlic and stir together. Add the lacinato kale in batches, letting the leaves wilt a bit before adding the next. Stir together and continue mixing until the greens start to soften. Remove from the heat and set aside.

In another large pot, heat the white wine, half the chopped parsley, and the halved garlic over medium heat. Add the clams. Cover and cook until all the clams have steamed open, 10 to 12 minutes. Remove the clams from the cooking liquid and pick the meat out. Strain the clam liquid and return the clams to the strained broth. Discard the empty shells and any clams that have not opened.

Add the chicken stock to the kale and return to medium heat. If you want more liquid, you can increase the amount of stock. Add the clams and remaining parsley. Season with salt and pepper. Pour in the chickpeas, stir together, and simmer over low heat until the kale is tender and the flavors have melded, 15 to 20 minutes. Serve immediately.

Storage: This soup freezes well. I freeze it in pint or quart containers, which makes it easier to thaw.

Our Christmas Eve Seafood Stew

Most coastal regions have some version of a fish stew: San Francisco has cioppino. Southern Italy has livornese. Tuscany has cacciucco. France has bouillabaisse. They're all slightly different dishes, but most of them are tomato based and all involve poaching seafood. What's different about this one, which I make on Christmas Eve, is that the squid and clams, along with the sofrito, give it an earthier base. There are tomatoes in the mix, but it isn't nearly as tomato-forward as the other stews.

In terms of what goes into the stew and in what proportions, it's up to you. When I make this dish for the Feast of the Seven Fishes, I usually omit any whitefish, as I do in this recipe. But if I'm making it during the summer, I'll throw in a few pieces of monkfish, after the clams, to make the stew even heartier. Regardless, serve this with crusty bread to sop up all the delicious flavors.

Serves 6 to 8

Kosher salt

1 whole lobster (1½ pounds), claws and tail separated, head reserved for another use, or 1 cup cooked lobster meat

2 cups Blond Sofrito (page 109)

1 cup white wine

One 28-ounce can whole peeled tomatoes

24 Manila or littleneck clams, cleaned and rinsed

2 pounds mussels, scrubbed and cleaned (see page 245)

Freshly ground black pepper

1 pound squid, cleaned, with bodies sliced into rings and tentacles halved

12 large (U10 or U12) head-on shrimp

8 large scallops

Grated zest and juice of ½ lemon

1 bunch parsley, roughly chopped

Crusty bread, for serving

Bring a large pot of salted water to a boil over medium-high heat. Add the lobster claws, then 2 minutes later add the tail. The claws should cook for 4 minutes total; the tail should cook for 2 minutes.

(recipe continues)

You want the lobster to be al dente as it will cook more in the sauce. Remove the lobster from the hot water and let cool.

When the lobster is cool enough to handle, remove the meat from the claws and tail, remove any cartilage, and roughly chop (you want to get about 1 cup). Set aside. Discard the shells and cartilage.

In a large wide pot or Dutch oven, warm the sofrito over low heat. Pour in the white wine, mix together, and season with salt. Add the tomatoes, crushing any larger chunks of tomato with your hands as you pour them in. Simmer slowly, stirring every so often, for about 1 hour.

Meanwhile, scrub the clams and mussels well.

After the stew has simmered for 1 hour, add the clams to the pot and cover. Wait for all clams to open, 8 to 12 minutes. Then add the mussels. Season with salt and pepper, and cook for another 8 to 10 minutes. If the clams and mussels fall out of their shells, remove the shells if needed to make more room in the pot. Remove and discard any that haven't opened.

Gently add the squid, shrimp, scallops, and lobster meat and stir to combine. Cover and continue to cook over low heat, gently stirring occasionally, until the seafood is no longer translucent, 10 to 15 minutes.

Stir in the lemon zest, lemon juice, and parsley. Continue cooking until all the seafood is cooked through, another 5 to 10 minutes. Be sure the pot is over low heat the entire time; you don't want the seafood to overcook. Season with salt and pepper and serve with bread alongside.

Blond Sofrito

Sofrito, an aromatic blend of cooking vegetables, wasn't part of my lexicon at all, but while Marco Canora was working at Craft, he left for a *stage* at Cibreo in Florence. When Marco returned, he came back praising the virtue of blond sofrito. We thought: Sofrito? We sent you to Florence and *this* is what you come back with, a basic flavor base? But soon Marco was adding it to many of the fish and light meat preparations, such as the Star-Spangled Squid Rice (page 251), and we were similarly won over. (We use a darker sofrito, which contains carrots, for darker meats.) Thanks in large part to Marco, the soul of Craft was more Italian than anything else. In fact, when the restaurateur Sirio Maccioni of Le Cirque came in with his wife, Egidiana, she pulled me aside and said, "This is the best Italian restaurant in the city." I'm not saying that's all because of this sofrito, but it didn't hurt.

Makes 3¼ cups

6 celery stalks, roughly chopped	2 cups extra-virgin olive oil
1 large fennel bulb, roughly chopped	1 large onion, finely chopped (see Note)

In a food processor, combine the celery, fennel, and ½ cup of the olive oil. Blend together until finely chopped.

Pour the remaining 1½ cups olive oil into a large pot and set over medium-low heat. Add the fennel/celery mixture and the onion. Gently stir. Cook over low heat until the vegetables are very soft and lightly caramelized, 50 minutes to 1 hour 10 minutes. Loosely cover with a lid to keep the mixture from splattering if needed.

Storage: Use immediately, or cool and refrigerate for up to 1 week or freeze for up to 6 months.

Note: Don't be tempted to chop the onion in the food processor, too; it gets mushy. It needs to be chopped by hand.

Cod with Leeks, Lemon Confit, and Olives

This recipe was a mainstay of my family's Christmas Day meal when I was growing up. I started making this, and all of our Christmas favorites, on Christmas Eve after I split with Dante's mom, since he spent Christmas Eve with me and Christmas Day with her. Christmas Eve—surrounded by family and loved ones—is still Dante's favorite meal of the year. The recipe starts with just one ingredient—here a nice loin of cod—and then layers on the flavors.

Serves 4

3 leeks, dark greens removed, white and light-green parts halved lengthwise
Kosher salt and freshly ground black pepper
1 cup extra-virgin olive oil, or as needed
1½ to 2 pounds cod fillet

¼ cup pieces Lemon Confit (page 112)
¼ cup cloves Garlic Confit (page 113)
4 sprigs fresh thyme
¼ cup pitted oil-cured black olives

Preheat the oven to 350°F.

In a medium baking dish, arrange the leeks in a single layer. Season with salt and pepper and add just enough olive oil to barely cover the leeks. Bake in the oven until the leeks are soft, about 30 minutes.

Remove the leeks from the oven. Season both sides of the cod generously with salt and add to the baking dish. Top with the lemon confit, garlic confit, and thyme. Cover the dish with foil, return it to the oven, and bake until the cod flesh is opaque, 25 to 30 minutes.

Serve the cod topped with the olives.

Lemon Confit

Lemon, tart though it is, can be easily pushed between savory and sweet. This versatility is one of this fruit's charms. But if you're looking to apply the bright acidic flavor to a savory preparation, lemon confit will get you there quickly. Like Oven-Roasted Tomatoes (page 117), this is both a recipe and an ingredient. Chopped up with parsley, it is a condiment to use with everything. It adds zing to a braise or to a sauce. Whisked together with some lightly sautéed garlic and olive oil, it's a simple elegant pasta sauce (and even better with anchovy).

Makes about 4 cups

6 small lemons (about 1½ pounds total)

½ cup minced shallots (2 to 3 shallots)

3 garlic cloves, minced (2 tablespoons)

⅓ cup kosher salt

3 tablespoons sugar

1 cup extra-virgin olive oil, for storage

Bring a large pot of water to a boil over high heat.

Add the lemons to the boiling water and blanch, just until the waxy top layer of the lemons softens, 1 to 2 minutes. Drain, rinse under cold water, and wipe the lemons clean. Dry the lemons and slice into very thin rings. Remove the ends and discard any seeds.

In a bowl, combine the shallots and garlic. In another bowl, mix together the salt and sugar. In a widemouthed 1-quart canning jar, arrange a layer of lemon rings. Sprinkle with some of the shallot/garlic mixture, followed by some of the salt/sugar mixture. Keep layering until all the lemons are used. The final layer should be salt and sugar. Cover the jar and refrigerate for 5 days, turning occasionally.

Storage: Confit can be used immediately or covered in olive oil and stored in the fridge for about 1 month.

Garlic Confit

Garlic confit is a shortcut to flavor. It's one of those prepared ingredients that, in the heat of service or just a time-pressed dinner at home, makes you thank your earlier self for thinking of it. We make huge batches of garlic confit at the restaurant, but at home, I often just keep a little pot of olive oil and garlic on top of the oven when I'm cooking and let it slowly and gently simmer. Like its brothers, Lemon Confit (at left) and Oven-Roasted Tomatoes (page 117), garlic confit deepens the flavor of braises, roasts, and pastas. If I'm braising a piece of meat, toward the end of cooking, I'll smash some garlic confit into the top of it before basting it. If I'm making myself a snack of hummus and pita, I'll fold some garlic confit into the hummus for a sweet and not too sharp garlic flavor. The same goes for Aioli (page 253).

Makes 2 cups

2 cups peeled garlic cloves   2 cups extra-virgin olive oil
(20 to 30)

In a small saucepan, combine the garlic and olive oil and warm over medium-low heat. When the first bubbles appear, reduce the heat to the lowest possible setting to stop the oil from bubbling. Cook until the garlic is very soft, about 40 minutes.

Allow the confit to cool to room temperature. Transfer it to a clean jar and refrigerate.

Storage: The confit will keep in the refrigerator for up to 2 weeks.

A Chicken That Tastes Like Rabbit

This recipe began as a very complicated dish I made at Mondrian.
It was a loin of rabbit plus a frenched rack stuffed with potato
chips—made by stuffing a blanched potato with pommes purées
and then frying it until it's crispy—and served with a rabbit kidney
on a rosemary skewer. The cooks hated making the dish, especially
the one guy whose job it was to make the chips. Little by little,
we started simplifying things, removing as many elements as we
possibly could while keeping what made it so delicious: the sauce.
Thanks to the soppressata, confits, olives, and roasted tomatoes, the
sauce has a bracing acidity and layers of deep flavor. Eventually, by
the time my Small Batch restaurant came around, what was rabbit
had become a braised chicken. But the chicken is really just an excuse
to sop up as much of the sauce as possible, which is why I often serve
this with polenta.

Serves 4

6 bone-in, skin-on chicken
   thighs (about 2½ pounds total)
Kosher salt and freshly ground
   black pepper
4 tablespoons extra-virgin
   olive oil
⅓ cup chopped soppressata
½ medium onion, diced
10 cherry tomatoes
1 cup dry white wine

4 pieces Lemon Confit
   (page 112), chopped
5 cloves Garlic Confit (page 113),
   chopped
10 oil-cured black olives, pitted
   and crushed
8 Oven-Roasted Tomatoes
   (page 117), chopped
1 cup chicken stock
4 sprigs fresh thyme

Preheat the oven to 325°F.

Pat the chicken thighs dry and season with salt and pepper. In a large
ovenproof skillet, heat 1 tablespoon of the olive oil over medium heat.
Add the chicken thighs skin-side down and cook until nicely golden
and crisp, 6 to 8 minutes. Flip and cook the bone side for 2 minutes.

(recipe continues)

Remove the seared chicken thighs from the pan and set aside on a plate.

Pour out the fat and add the remaining 3 tablespoons olive oil and the soppressata. Cook over medium heat, stirring occasionally, until the soppressata has rendered the majority of its fat and begun to crisp up slightly, 2 to 3 minutes.

Add the onion and cook until translucent, about 3 minutes. Add the cherry tomatoes, increase the heat to medium-high, and cook until slightly blistered, 2 to 3 minutes.

Pour the white wine into the pan to deglaze, scraping up the bits that have collected at the bottom of the pan. Cook until the sauce has reduced and thickened, about 8 minutes.

Add the lemon confit, garlic confit, crushed olives, and roasted tomatoes. Reduce the heat to medium, season with salt and pepper, and cook until the ragout mixture has reduced slightly, about 5 minutes.

Return the browned chicken thighs to the pan. Pour in just enough stock so that the thighs are mostly submerged but the skin is exposed. Add the thyme sprigs.

Transfer the pan to the oven and bake until the sauce has reduced slightly and the chicken skin is crisp and the meat is tender, 45 minutes to 1 hour. Serve immediately.

Oven-Roasted Tomatoes

Tomatoes, one of my favorite and most often used ingredients, can be tricky to cook with. They put out a lot of liquid, waterlogging everything from sauces to roasts. During the relatively short peak summer season, tomatoes are abundant and undeniably delicious. But out of season, they can be shockingly flavorless. Oven-roasting a tomato is a way around this. Roasting the tomatoes extracts enough flavor from even off-peak tomatoes that the tomato essence comes through. (Of course, this works well with peak-season tomatoes, too!) Slow cooking the tomatoes removes their water, which makes them easier to use in a variety of ways. I use this preparation on its own and as an ingredient: In a pasta, with basil. With a roast, in the liquid. On toast, with ricotta. If I have extra, I put them in a mason jar, cover them in olive oil, and keep them for up to a month, though they're so versatile they rarely last that long.

Makes about 4 cups

15 Roma tomatoes (4 pounds total), halved lengthwise

Kosher salt and freshly ground black pepper

1 head garlic, cloves separated and left unpeeled

6 to 8 sprigs fresh thyme

½ to ¾ cup extra-virgin olive oil (depending on size of pan)

Position a rack in the bottom third of the oven and preheat the oven to 350°F.

Generously season the tomatoes with salt and pepper. Arrange them skin-side up in a large roasting pan or on a sheet pan. Scatter the garlic and thyme over top of the tomatoes and drizzle generously with olive oil. The oil should reach about one-third of the way up the tomatoes.

Bake until the tomatoes appear slightly shrunken and cooked, about 1 hour.

(recipe continues)

Remove the tomatoes from the oven and let cool before peeling away and discarding the tomato and garlic skins and the thyme sprigs.

Storage: Store the tomatoes, garlic, and juices in an airtight container in the refrigerator for up to 1 week, under oil for a month, or in the freezer for up to 6 months.

Duck Breast, Pan-Roasted

Cooking duck brings me right back to my days at the Hôtel de France in Gascony, duck and foie gras capital of the world. There's a tremendous variety of ducks to choose from, each with its own flavor profile. On Long Island, where I live, by far the most common duck is the Pekin duck, which was brought to the States in the late nineteenth century. Though there are more flavorful ducks, Pekin duck has a nice amount of fat, which means that the relatively lean meat is kept moist even as it is cooked through. (This is especially important when roasting a whole duck.) This recipe takes advantage of all that delicious rendered fat by using it to cook the vegetables. The result is an immensely flavorful and comforting winter meal.

Serves 2

2 Pekin duck breasts (9 ounces each)

Kosher salt

1 apple, cored and sliced into ⅛-inch wedges

1 large leek, white parts only, thinly sliced

1 small fennel bulb, halved and thinly sliced

1-inch knob fresh ginger, peeled and thinly sliced

Freshly ground black pepper

½ cup chestnuts, roasted and peeled

2 sprigs fresh thyme

2 sprigs fresh rosemary

1 tablespoon honey

1 tablespoon apple cider vinegar or honey vinegar

With a sharp paring knife, score the fat of the duck breasts in a tight (about ¼ inch) crisscross pattern. Season both sides of the breasts generously with salt.

Put the duck breasts skin-side down in a cold sauté pan. Set over medium-low heat and allow the duck fat to render and the skin to get golden and crisp, about 15 minutes.

Flip the breasts and cook for another 3 to 4 minutes for medium, or until the internal temperature reads 130° to 140°F. Remove the breasts from the pan and let them rest. Pour out all but 3 tablespoons duck fat (reserve this delicious fat for another use).

Return the pan to medium heat and add the apple, leek, fennel, and ginger. Season with salt and pepper. Cook, stirring occasionally, until the apple and vegetables begin to soften, 3 to 4 minutes.

Add the chestnuts, thyme, and rosemary and continue to cook until the apple and vegetables are nearly soft and the flavors have melded, 3 to 4 minutes.

Add the honey and vinegar, stirring to coat. Continue to cook until the apple and vegetables are soft and caramelized, another 2 to 3 minutes.

Slice the duck breast into ½-inch slices and spoon the apple mixture alongside. Serve immediately.

Sunday Gravy
with Meatballs and Braciole

Every Sunday my mother made us Sunday Gravy, a hearty meat-filled tomato ragu. Every family I knew had its own version, which like this one changed through the generations. For instance, my mother didn't use ricotta in her meatballs, but I do. After church, my brothers and I would crowd into the kitchen as my mom fried the meatballs and gave us a couple before they went into the pot of tomatoes, as a snack. Later that evening, the entire family would assemble for a dinner of meatballs, gravy (never "sauce"), and macaroni, which is what we called pasta. Call it whatever you want, but this recipe works best with a dried macaroni shape, such as a ziti or rigatoni, which can stand up to the hearty gravy. You can add pork shoulder with the bone still on to reinforce the gravy. But if you really like braciole, add more braciole.

Serves 6 to 8/makes 12 meatballs and 4 braciole

MEATBALLS
1 pound ground beef
1 pound ground pork
Kosher salt
½ cup freshly grated pecorino cheese
½ cup freshly grated Parmesan cheese
6 garlic cloves, chopped
½ pound ricotta cheese
Freshly ground black pepper
4 large eggs, whisked
½ cup chopped fresh parsley
5 tablespoons extra-virgin olive oil

TOMATO SAUCE
Two 28-ounce cans peeled whole tomatoes, hand-crushed
Two 28-ounce cans crushed tomatoes
Kosher salt
2 tablespoons extra-virgin olive oil
2 to 3 pounds sweet Italian sausage, depending on how many you're serving

BRACIOLE
1 cup chopped fresh parsley
¼ cup fresh bread crumbs

(ingredients continue on next page)

2 tablespoons freshly grated
Parmesan or pecorino cheese

3 garlic cloves, chopped

Kosher salt and freshly ground
black pepper

4 tablespoons extra-virgin
olive oil

1 pound flank steak, cut into
4 pieces, each pounded to ¼ to
⅛ inch thick (see Note)

TO FINISH

½ cup red wine

3 sprigs fresh basil (or fresh
tomato leaves)

Kosher salt and freshly ground
black pepper

2 pounds rigatoni or pasta shape
of choice

Freshly grated pecorino cheese,
for serving

Make the meatballs: In a large bowl, combine the ground beef and pork and season liberally with salt. Add the pecorino, Parmesan, and garlic and mix everything together (I use my hands to do this). Add the ricotta and mix again. Season with LOTS of pepper. Mix together again. Using your hands or a large wooden spoon, mix the eggs and parsley into the meat mixture.

Check for seasoning (this step isn't required, but it's helpful): In a small skillet, heat 1 tablespoon of the olive oil over medium heat. Make a 1-inch meatball and place it in the pan. Brown the meatball on all sides until cooked through, about 5 minutes. Let cool slightly, then taste and adjust the seasoning to the meat mixture as needed.

When you're pleased with the seasoning, form the mixture into 12 roughly 2-inch meatballs. You can place the meatballs on a sheet of parchment as you roll them.

Working in batches, pour 2 tablespoons of the olive oil into a heavy-bottomed skillet and place it over medium-low heat. When the oil is hot, add half the meatballs and brown them on all sides, 10 to 12 minutes total. Repeat with the remaining meatballs and the remaining 2 tablespoons olive oil.

Make the tomato sauce: Pour all the tomatoes into a large Dutch oven (or other large pot) that will ultimately be able to hold all the sauce, meatballs, sausages, and braciole. Add 1 cup water to one of the tomato cans and swirl out any remaining juices. Then use the same water for the remaining cans, and add that liquid to the pot as well. Season the tomatoes with salt. Bring to a low simmer over low heat, then add the browned meatballs to the tomato sauce.

Wipe the skillet clean and return to medium heat. Pour in the oil, add the sausages, and brown on all sides, 7 to 10 minutes. Once browned, add the sausages to the tomato sauce. (You might need to cut your sausage into thirds to fit it into the pot.)

Make the braciole: On a wooden cutting board, place the parsley, bread crumbs, Parmesan, and garlic. Season generously with salt and pepper. Pour 2 tablespoons of the olive oil over everything. Use a knife to chop the parsley and garlic and scrape everything together to make a paste.

Lay the meat flat on a clean work surface. Spread 1 to 2 tablespoons of the parsley/bread crumb mixture over each piece of meat. Roll up the meat and tie closed with butcher's twine placed about 1 inch apart.

In a different pan (or clean the pan you browned the sausages in), heat the remaining 2 tablespoons olive oil over medium heat. Add the braciole and brown on all sides, 7 to 10 minutes. Transfer the browned braciole to the tomato sauce.

To finish: At this point, the sauce should be bubbling slowly over low heat. Add the red wine and basil and give it a stir. Let the sauce and meat cook together slowly for 3 to 4 hours. Use a large wooden spoon to occasionally stir the pot to make sure the bottom is not burning. Season with more salt and pepper as needed.

About 30 minutes before you're ready to eat, bring a large pot of salted water to a boil over high heat. Add the pasta and cook to al dente according to the package directions.

Drain the pasta and return it to the pot over low heat. Add some sauce to keep it from sticking. Your pasta shouldn't be oversauced.

(recipe continues)

125

Let the pasta and sauce cook gently over low heat to coat the pasta fully with the sauce.

Serve at the table with extra gravy and a bowl of the sausage, meatballs, and braciole alongside. Have some freshly grated pecorino on the table, too.

Note: Ask your butcher to cut and pound the flank steak for you.

Storage: Extra sauce and meat can be stored in an airtight container in the refrigerator for up to 4 days. It'll keep frozen (without pasta) for 4 to 6 months.

5

Flying High

GROWING UP, I could see New York City's skyline from my bedroom in Elizabeth. It loomed intimidatingly at the edges of my consciousness as I dove into cooking. I imagined that only the very elite made it there, people who'd studied in France under the Greats. So when I left for Manhattan in the summer of 1985 with printouts of my résumé in my backpack, I assumed I was a long shot at best. I'd probably get only one chance at this, and I was anxious I'd blow it.

From the moment Henri Soulé opened Le Pavillon at the 1939 World's Fair, French restaurants had become synonymous with fine dining in New York City, and they still held an iron grip. Restaurants like Lutèce, La Grenouille, Le Cirque, and La Côte Basque set the standard: formal service, bone china, fine linen. But a crop of American restaurateurs was slowly emerging, making the case that American cuisine could be fine dining, too. Their names were familiar to me from the pages of *Cuisine*—Larry Forgione, Barry Wine, Jonathan Waxman—and I had come to think of them as fellow travelers, achieving on a larger scale what Jerry and I had tried to pull off at 40 Main. Not to knock French cuisine (I, too, still worshipped at that altar), but with no formal training or introduction, I knew it wasn't happening for me. So it was to this young avant-garde that I looked. They were shaking things up in a distinctly American way that I found exciting.

I might have been scared, but I set my sights high. My first stop in the city was the Quilted Giraffe, arguably the hottest American restaurant in the country, which had just been awarded four stars in the *New York Times*. I left a résumé for the owner and chef, Barry Wine, and then headed to Jams, Jonathan Waxman's new restaurant on the Upper East Side. Since arriving from Santa Monica the year before, Waxman had made a splash as an apostle of produce-driven cuisine. He was young, like me, with a shaggy head of hair and a reputation as a fun guy. I thought I'd be a good fit. Sadly, the chef de cuisine, a nice woman named Helen Chardack, told me they were already fully staffed. "Go see this guy Alfred, downtown," she suggested. "I hear he's hiring." Alfred was Alfred Portale, her then husband, who had just taken over Gotham Bar & Grill on 12th Street. I made my way to the Village.

When I arrived at Gotham, Alfred had been there all of three days. The departing chef, Brendan Walsh, had a big name, but it hadn't worked out, and the place was in turmoil. Although Alfred hadn't yet gotten much in the way of press, he'd worked with the revered French chef Michel Guérard to open a buzzy café at Bloomingdale's. (Macy's had opened a sprawling gourmet market called the Cellar at Macy's in 1977, and Bloomingdale's was trying to catch up.) Even more impressively, Portale had worked in France with Guérard and the Troisgros brothers. All this to say: The man had credentials. Back in New York, he'd spent time on the line with Daniel Boulud, Thomas Keller, and David Bouley.

Alfred was dapper and methodical (and a great guy; we're still friends, forty years later). He would eventually emerge as a pioneer of presentation, using vertical space on the plate in a new way that suited the high-flying 1980s, but in those early days he was still grappling with Walsh's menu, trying to put his own stamp on it. A week later, I got a call out of the blue from Barry Wine, offering me a trial run in his kitchen. I weighed the risk, trading a guaranteed job for one that might not even materialize, but then the itch came slyly back: The food at Quilted was exciting and offbeat. I knew I'd be learning there. I felt bad telling Alfred I was leaving after a week. He wasn't happy, but he understood. After all, it was the Quilted Giraffe.

It's difficult to fully convey the frenzy—and divisiveness— that the Quilted Giraffe inspired back in 1985. Wine had opened the restaurant with his wife, Susan, in 1975 in their Victorian home in New Paltz, New York, then moved it to the city a few years later, taking over a former Greek diner on 2nd Avenue and 50th Street before moving to Madison Avenue. Barry wasn't a trained chef; in fact, he'd only assumed the role when his original chef had car trouble one night and didn't make it to work. After a career in corporate law, Barry had artistic aspirations and wanted to reinvent American fine dining along the lines of how he was reinventing himself—cheeky, eccentric, risk-taking. Technically speaking, Barry's food was as elevated as Lutèce's but without the stuffiness. The menu emphasized freshness and produce, like Waxman's, but in a louder, showier way that made sense given the ethos of the day.

When the Quilted Giraffe first arrived in New York, Mimi Sheraton, the influential *New York Times* critic, hated it, singling out such travesties as Barry's penchant for fruit in unlikely places, like his dish of lobster and monkfish in a cream sauce with cantaloupe balls and raspberries. Sheraton also lambasted the service, describing it as overbearing and embarrassing. But it hardly mattered. The restaurant caught the imagination of a city that was newly awash in Wall Street cash and appreciated such audacity after living through the dour pessimism of the late 1970s. And when Quilted got its four stars in 1984, a tsunami of adoration followed. Quilted was packed nightly with titans of finance, politicians, famous artists, and jet-setters, all rabid to try the signature caviar beggar's purses with gold leaf. Warren Beatty had a standing reservation, as did Jackie Onassis. It was the hottest ticket in town, by a mile.

Barry told me he didn't like to hire "career cooks" like me because he viewed them as dull pedants and rule followers. He preferred people who'd come to cooking later, like himself, unencumbered by muscle memory or stuffy doctrine. That's how his kitchen ended up filled with raw talent, like Noel Comess, a first-timer who went on to own Tom Cat Bakery, and Wayne Nish, who had owned a bunch of copy shops before deciding in his thirties to go to culinary school. When I got there, the only other career cooks were a flamboyant St. Lucian named Hillary Gregg, who hit on me nightly, and David Kinch, a sweet guy who ran the vegetable station.

For all his idiosyncrasies, Barry ruled his kitchen with a militant precision that was new to me and ahead of its time. He was the first to place digital clocks everywhere, as his theory was you can't screw up much in under ten minutes. Every entrée was prepared in precisely ten minutes (with the exception of lamb, which took twelve), and there was hell to pay if you fell behind, since it sent a cascade of woe down the line. My job that week was to trail and assist a cook at the sauté station named Marcie Barker.

Maybe because I stood closer to him and was in his sightline, or perhaps it was some sort of a test, but whenever Marcie would slip, even by thirty seconds, Barry would yell at me, not her: "New guy, get your food up on time!" I knew better than to talk back, but there wasn't much I could do—it was Marcie's show. This happened the next night, and the one after that, as I stood like a schmuck, frustrated and helpless. Finally, at the beginning of service on Friday, I asked Marcie to let me run the station that night. If I wasn't getting the job, I'd like it to be because I screwed up, not her. Marcie stepped aside and let me have at it. The dishes flew out every ten minutes. Barry offered me a job.

The kitchen culture at Quilted was ahead of its time, too. Almost everyone working there was a college graduate, and Barry hired women as readily as men, a real rarity in top kitchens then, when sexism was still open and rampant. There was a blissful sanity to the place, quite possibly due to the women, who brought more professionalism and less ass-grabbing to the job. Or maybe it was because Barry's concept of the schedule was formed by his years in corporate law, with its five-day week. He liked to spend weekends at his farm in New Paltz, so we were closed on Saturdays and Sundays. We were also only open for dinner, making for a shorter workday (ten hours, instead of the usual twelve to fourteen). That five-day week allowed us to really focus on our jobs without the messy role-swapping of a seven-day-a-week restaurant, with its

On the line at the Quilted Giraffe, 1986

overlapping shifts. That, plus the absence of exhaustion, freed us up to focus and play.

I quickly adapted to Barry's system. I loved his unorthodox way with vegetables. Unlike the menus I'd worked with up until then, where each dish had its "set," Barry kept twenty or so seasonal vegetables blanched and at the ready. As orders came in, David would heat them gently in beurre fondue, a melted emulsion of butter and water, and hand them off to Barry, who would toss and combine them in novel ways. It felt freeing, as did Barry's rule forbidding parties larger than four, which removed the stress that comes with timing a giant table. To my surprise, I found that the orderly flow, the regularity and consistency of it, could calm my noisy mind in much the same way chaos once had. Some of the lessons I'd gained at less illustrious joints were now serving me well; I sped through my prep (thank you, Evelyn's), which gave me time to help out in other stations or even break down a whole baby lamb when it came through our doors (here's looking at you, Chestnut Tavern). Most importantly, though, I was learning. Clearly it was working out for Barry, too, because within a few months, he made me sous-chef.

I was flying high, and not just from the work. Regi and I, always off and on, were off at this point, and, newly single, I began palling around with a new friend, Yves Picot, son of the seasoned restaurateurs Jean-Paul and Monique Picot of the midtown bistro La Bonne Soupe. Yves had grown up in the city and clambered easily through its shadow spaces as only a city kid could. After our shift, we'd hit King Tut's Wah Wah Hut in the East Village and from there move on to the Pyramid Club to dance. Next up was Save the Robots, an underground club that relocated nightly to different warehouses—half the fun was tracking it down. Yves introduced me to New Wave music, and we'd go to Danceteria, or the Tunnel, fueled by the Bolivian marching powder that powered the entire ecosystem of New York City's downtown in those days. I was twenty-four and hell-bent on experiencing all of it. Sleep was an afterthought.

After one Friday shift that summer, Yves invited me out for an impromptu weekend at his parents' farmhouse in Southampton. We left right from work and showed up in the wee hours when everyone was asleep. I woke up charmed to find myself in a bright bedroom overlooking the pool. The place was no mansion, but it was beautiful and sure seemed like one to me. Downstairs, a loaf of fresh crusty bread and some good cheese awaited us, along with plush towels by the pool. There was a gracious informality to it all, and I realized I was experiencing true hospitality—not the transactional kind you'd find in a restaurant, but the kind that served as an expression of who my hosts were and how they welcomed others warmly into their lives. It made an impression.

After a languorous day in the sun, we showered off and met at the pool for pre-dinner drinks. I was wearing the outfit I'd arrived in—jeans and a vest over my sleeveless shirt (it was the '80s; don't judge). Monique discreetly whispered something to Yves and he yanked me upstairs and handed me a collared shirt from his closet, explaining that my usual uniform wouldn't cut it for dinner. Smarting with embarrassment, I threw it on and returned to the party, where I saw food journalists Bryan Miller and Craig Claiborne, both luminaries of the culinary world and writer heroes of mine, drinks in hand.

That night, as if it was the most natural thing in the world, I was folded into an urbane circle I had never imagined, and they acted like it was the most natural thing in the world to have me there. It was heady stuff. At the same time, as the conversation toggled between English and French, I struggled to follow along, feeling out of my depth and acutely aware of my humble origins in a way I'd never been before. Cooking was gaining me entry into a rarified space, but I lacked the tools (or so I believed) to navigate it. What to wear, how to speak, which fork to use—there seemed to be a code that some people were born knowing, like a club with invisible admission policies. All at once, I was awash in that old insecurity from my school days, feeling the shame of not measuring up, and if I'm honest, it's a feeling that lives in me still, closer to the surface than I like to admit. To this day I take great care with my clothes—Lori teases me about it—and I'd bet that weekend at the Picots' is the reason why.

Professionally, though, my confidence was at an all-time high. Which is probably why, a year later, when Dan Cannizzo called to offer me the top job at 40 Main Street, I gave it serious thought. On the one hand, the Quilted Giraffe was as exalted a place as New York had to offer. But as fast as my ascent there had been, I was never going to be the chef: The restaurant was Barry Wine's brainchild, the product of his and Susan's vision. It was clear to me that if I was going to be a chef—a real one—I'd need to develop a personal vision of my own, preferably away from the glaring heat lamps of New York City. Cannizzo's 40 Main Street could give me that chance.

And yet, the thought of 40 Main without Jerry felt all wrong. It was ours, something we had built together. I told Dan I'd take the gig, but only if Jerry returned as co-chef. Jerry had spent the year in Los Angeles, studying under Wolfgang Puck at Chinois on Main, and apparently he had said the same thing about me. The Tom and Jerry show was back on.

Jerry and I hit the ground running, immediately back in our groove. This time around, rather than ideating a menu and then shopping for it, we began with the ingredients. The seasons told us which products should lead, as did our access to quality from nearby farms and markets—if it was fresh, we'd take a humble monkfish over an exotic lobster tail that was shipped to us frozen. "Seasonal" and "market driven" are such ubiquitous terms today that they're nearly meaningless, but in 1986, that kind of approach was still new. From a restaurant standpoint, spontaneity is harder to pull off than a set plan. But given where Jerry and I were creatively, we couldn't have done it any other way.

We were maniacal about ingredients. We lost sleep over them. Literally. Two or three times a week, Jerry and I would pile into Crash's station wagon at 3 a.m. and drive to the Fulton Fish Market, a bustling open-air giant in lower Manhattan with stalls filling the space from South Street to Water Street right under FDR Drive. This was twenty years before the market decamped to Hunt's Point in the Bronx, and it was a grimy place, with bloodied ice melting underfoot and groups of rough-looking guys huddled over barrel fires to smoke and keep warm. The market was controlled by the Genovese family, who charged sellers for protection and buyers like us for "parking." If you wanted to get home with your fish—and your tires—you paid. We'd been introduced around by Mike Marino, a fish supplier in New Jersey who knew my parents from the Gran Centurions, so the sellers took care of us. Jerry and I would touch the whole snappers and sea bass in their crates, feeling for firmness and spring under the skin, turning away any with bruises or soft spots. We'd check the eyes—if they weren't still bulging and clear, we'd move on. Once we'd chosen, we'd refuse the fish if the fishmongers threw it roughly onto the scale, and they came to see that Jerry and I were a different breed than their usual customers. Soon they were setting aside choice specimens for us and handling them with care. There was one other chef back then also braving the inky predawn market, fingering the gills and haggling with sellers. It was a young Gilbert Le Coze, who had just brought his Paris restaurant, Le Bernardin, to New York with his sister, Maguy. We'd nod collegially at our fellow zealot and carry on.

From the fish market, Jerry and I would drive thirty blocks or so north to the Meatpacking District, where we could scrutinize lamb loins and veal racks hanging on the transoms lining Washington Street. It would still be dark out, and the meatpackers weren't the only ones hustling. Take a wrong turn and you'd stumble on another rough trade: hookers of every stripe and flavor, walking, waiting, sliding into backseats. It

---

was a tough and ugly place—not somewhere to linger. If you would have told me that in twenty years the area would be filled with boutiques and brunch spots, or that for a time my young family would call the neighborhood home, I would have been shocked.

From the Meatpacking District we'd head back through the Lincoln Tunnel to D'Artagnan, in Jersey City, a small two-person business that had exclusive access to incredibly high-quality foie gras from New York's Hudson Valley. The owners, Ariane Daguin and George Faison, were great people, and their setup was a far cry from the renowned, international operation it would one day become. Back then they ran the business from a single walk-in, settling accounts on a door propped up on milk crates. Jerry and I would scoop up ducks, quail, and foie gras and drive back to Millburn with the sun coming up in our rear window. We'd unload our haul, catch a few hours of sleep, and then roll back in to prep service.

Jerry and I fell into an easy rhythm. We loved being together, and we were doing great work. Jerry wasn't just a talented chef; he was also a whiz at management, costing out recipes, working out schedules—all the things my ADHD brain dreaded. It left me with the time and space to focus on flavors and presentation, the work of finding my voice as a chef. This was the moment when diners became interested in the faces behind the swinging door, and we were expected to interact with guests. Jerry was naturally shy and preferred to stay in the back of the house, so I'd throw on a clean apron and walk into the dining room to chat. Like my father, I was social when I needed to be, and even enjoyed it. I didn't know it at the time, but Jerry and the rest called me Hollywood Colicchio. Little did they (or I) know.

6.

Painting the Town

DAN CANNIZZO'S PARTNERS were giving him a hard time. Two chefs cost more than one, our food costs were high, and worst of all, thanks to New Jersey's arcane liquor laws, they couldn't get a liquor license, closing off a major source of revenue. Dan gave me and Jerry the bad news: One of us would have to go.

Predictably, neither of us was willing to sacrifice the other, so we both gave notice. I pondered my options. Could I find a chef job of my own? Try to arrange a *stage* in France? Like a lot of people with ADHD (though I still had no clue that's what I was working with), I relied on urgency and nightly deadlines to kick myself into gear. Breaking down the steps necessary to undertake either of these possibilities felt overwhelming. The obvious thing to do, therefore, was to procrastinate and party.

Procrastinating became easier when Alfred Portale reached out asking for a favor. His sous-chefs were slacking, and he needed someone on the line to goose them along. I didn't relish being the heavy, but I agreed to take the job while I figured out my next steps.

It was a mistake from the start. I resented the step backward to line cook, and it showed in my shitty attitude. I got the work done, but I made no friends doing it. I wasn't open to learning anything, and the plunge from a job that had offered autonomy and a creative outlet to one where I was effectively policing other people—in service of someone else's food—wasn't good for my psyche. Looking back, I can see how closely this mirrored my father's experience after he lost his barbershop. Back then, his disappointment spiraled into an ever-worsening gambling problem. My disappointment, too, needed to be channeled somewhere, so I sought out other thrills.

Regi and I, after a brief reconciliation, were now done for good. She'd taken up with the stable, decent guy she would go on to marry, and our apartment in East Orange felt desolate. My brothers were both getting on with their lives—Mike was becoming a CPA and dating Sue, his warm and lovely future wife, and Phil was playing point guard on the basketball team at Kean College. My parents loved me, but being in Elizabeth offered no solace. I was bored and lonely and had time on my hands, a toxic combination. My habitual itch for novelty had begun to widen and darken into something else—a hunt for greater and greater thrills to drown out the inner noise of my falling self-regard. I didn't realize it at the time, but I was sliding into depression.

So I self-medicated, as I had in those crummy feel-bad high school years. After-shift drinks with the other cooks would lead to shots, and then out would come the weed or some pills. But these were mere appetizers—the main course was cocaine, plentiful and ubiquitous in 1980s New York City, and a quick fix for my growing malaise. I told myself I was having fun (I wasn't). There was no one waiting for me at home; I had no restaurant to wake up and run; I had no larger purpose guiding me. But when I was high, I didn't need to think. So my friends and I painted the town, indulging whenever and wherever we could. The shenanigans of a bunch of young idiot chefs raised no eyebrows. If anything, we were welcomed like rock stars. Years later, books and articles about us would celebrate these lost years as the stuff of legend. After Anthony Bourdain's tragic suicide in 2018, Lori published an article on *Medium* called "The Bad Boy Chef" that delved into this phenomenon:

> Kitchens naturally select for young people who prefer action over academics. It's an environment where ADHD is an asset, where a busy, multi-tasking brain pushes one up the ladder, rather than down. But kitchens are also frenetic spaces where emotional pain goes overlooked and unsupported, fueling depression, anxiety, and low self-esteem. Enter drugs and alcohol, which lift the negative self-talk just long enough to rinse and repeat. The "bad boy" fiction reinforces this toxic cycle: *Power through, young man. Pain is for pussies.*

And power through I did. I was a study in perfect solipsism. After a night of partying, barely able to stand, I'd climb on my Suzuki motorcycle with little thought for my own safety (or anyone else's) and gun it for home, mistaking the hairpin turns and the wind in my face for freedom. If someone then had suggested therapy or medication— the things that might have actually helped me—I would have laughed in their face and told them to lighten up. My wake-up call came one late summer afternoon in 1987. I woke up clammy and sick on my sofa, with blood caked down my front, hardened like a bib on my T-shirt.

I had no memory of getting home the night before; the last thing I remembered was visiting a shady fifth-floor walkup in Harlem to score some coke with a cook I barely liked named Louis. I stumbled my way into the bathroom and snapped on the light. A bleary lowlife I didn't recognize was looking at me from the mirror: eyes swollen, jaw sore from grinding. I realized then and there I had to make a change. The way I was going, if I didn't die first, I'd end up some also-ran, washed up before I'd even made my mark. My parents hadn't raised me to be this person.

Looking back now, I see just how callously I took my own life (and other people's) in my hands. That I was self-medicating against some inner shame is no excuse. But I was lucky: I only surfed the knife's edge of addiction and never was fully sucked into its undertow. Many others of my generation weren't as fortunate. Today there are a number of chefs I admire who have come forward to share their stories of addiction and recovery, bravely addressing the mental health issues we've spent too long as an industry ignoring. Andrew Zimmern, Gregory Gourdet, and Sean Brock come to mind, though there are many others. Thanks to them, and organizations like Southern Smoke Foundation, the restaurant business is finally taking substance abuse seriously as an industry hazard and interrogating the toxic tropes of masculinity and excess that have kept so many of us from getting the help we need.

What saved me wasn't wisdom or willpower. I had neither. It was a phone call from Ariane Daguin of D'Artagnan. Some weeks earlier I had asked if her father, the acclaimed Gascon chef André Daguin, might take me on for a *stage* in France. A *stage* (rhymes with *raj*) is an internship in an established French kitchen, usually unpaid, that gives a young cook the chance to gain valuable experience. It was (and remains) an important way for cooks to burnish their résumés in an industry in which kitchen lineage lends more credibility than a fancy degree. Ariane called to say her father was willing to set me up for three months at Hôtel de France, his Michelin-starred restaurant and inn in Gascony, the foie gras capital of the world. If I performed well, he'd make an introduction to chefs in Paris so I could continue my training there. I was being offered a lifeline and I grabbed it.

Gascony is wedged in the southwest corner of France, between the Atlantic Ocean and the Garonne River, which runs from Bordeaux down to the Pyrenees. Its proximity to the Spanish border probably accounts for its Basque-like vibe, immortalized in the character of D'Artagnan, the most stubbornly romantic of the three musketeers. Culinarily, the region (an imprecise term, as it loosely enfolds parts of two official regions, Nouvelle-Aquitaine and Occitanie) is known for its Armagnac and its abundance of wild game and fowl.

I arrived in France in August 1987 with my guitar, my knife roll, and a few hundred dollars my family had pressed upon me at my going-away party. I spoke no French, and therefore the cooks regarded me—the mute American *stagier*—with that uniquely Gallic mix of indifference and contempt reserved for non-French speakers. I was given a room under the roof, stowed my things, and was immediately put to work.

I was excited to be there. André Daguin was a legend; the man had singlehandedly made Gascony an important culinary destination, not by drawing visitors to its picturesque countryside with Paris-style food but by unapologetically elevating and amplifying its native ingredients. André's son, Arnaud, was the chef de cuisine, in charge of day-to-day operations. Arnaud was tall and handsome, with a handlebar mustache. He was only a few years older than me but already a bit of a playboy. Under him was Pascal Barbot, the sous-chef, a talent in his own right. I was quickly assigned the most menial prep work, from meticulously hand-cleaning crates of woodsy cèpes to singeing the feathers off wild pigeons. I was at the very bottom of the ladder, but I didn't care because I was seeing ingredients and techniques I'd never encountered before. I was learning.

The menu featured an amazing array of game birds, all new to me, like thumb-sized alouettes, cooked on skewers and eaten crispy and whole, and palombes, majestic wild pigeons that were roasted and served rare. André was famous for his steaklike preparation of the rich and gamy Magret duck, the "rib eye of the sky," which was plentiful in Gascony, and a far cry from its milder and more refined Parisian cousin, the Muscovy. Working with these foods didn't just change me as a cook, it grew my palate as an eater. (To this day I'll take a chewy, flavorful strip steak over a tender but bland filet mignon, and I'll always order a squab.)

But what really got my attention was the foie gras, which was of a quality I had never seen. In American restaurants, there's a preciousness to how foie gras is prepared. But at the Hôtel de France it was a staple, and the chefs treated it with the same robust confidence they brought to everything else. Dozens of livers would roll through the door each day, and it was my job to carefully clean and devein the lobes before handing them off to Arnaud and his crew. They'd marinate some in sugar, salt, and Armagnac, then Cryovac and stuff them into a terrine mold to be cooked in a low steam oven. A second terrine might be seasoned with roasted tomato, and a third with a confit of shallot and garlic. After chilling, all three would be delicately sliced and served, riffing off one another on the same plate.

Or they'd hard-boil a portion of foie gras in stock, serving the surviving morsel over sautéed leeks with a few spoonfuls of the *cuisson* (cooking liquid) over the top. Or they'd season the liver with nothing more than salt, pepper, and a bit of sugar, then Cryovac and cold-cure it in the freezer for months, before shaving it over greens. André leaned into the inherent qualities of each ingredient with a lusty naturalism I admired. To him, even the yellow fat that I'd learned to cut away as the foie gras cooked was something to be enjoyed, and he'd incorporate it, too, into a dish. Things like this shook up my understanding of French food.

I quickly established a routine. From my small room on the top floor, I'd head to the butler's pantry for a quick cup of coffee and a croissant, then make my way into the kitchen by 8 a.m. I'd get my own prep done, and then, restless as ever, I'd look around for ways to be useful, hoping to nudge my way onto the line. It's easy to be humble (never my strong suit) when you don't speak the language, and in time I earned the cooks' grudging respect, especially after I volunteered to skin a whole wild hare—a grisly job no one else particularly wanted. I visualized the photos of Jacques Pépin skinning a rabbit in his book *La Methode* and went for it. My efforts paid off: When Arnaud went on vacation, Pascal let me slide into his spot at the roast station. Life got even better with the arrival of another American, Kerry Heffernan, who showed up after a stint working for David Bouley. He was whip-smart, also listened to Echo and the Bunnymen, and, best of all, spoke English, so I had someone to talk to. To this day he is one of my best friends.

As our time at Hôtel de Paris came to a close, Arnaud agreed to set up *stages* for us in Paris. Kerry and I could hardly wait—I'm sure we imagined we'd set those Paris kitchens on fire—but we were met there by Arnaud, hangdog and apologizing. It seems we'd become pawns in an angry family dispute. For reasons unknown, mère and père Daguin strongly objected to the fiancée Arnaud had brought home from vacation, and André decided to teach his arrogant son a lesson. He called around Paris, telling his peers not to hire "Arnaud's Americans." Sure enough, no one would hire us. Kerry and I were crestfallen, but in the way of twenty-somethings, we quickly rebounded. Kerry had already done one *stage* in Paris and had friends in high places (aka fifth-floor flats), so we couch-surfed for a few weeks with them, eating our way around. We couldn't afford too many high-end places, but we made it to Alain Senderens's three-Michelin-starred Lucas Carton and to La Coupole in Montparnasse. The best part of Paris was the food shops, the cheese shops, and the boulangeries. Even on a modest budget, we ate like kings. After a few weeks of this, I ran out of cash and headed home.

Spring
Recipes

Mortadella with Fava Beans, Celery, Rhubarb, and Blood Orange Vinaigrette

The first time I made this salad was in Mattituck, as a way to utilize some pickled watermelon rind I had from the year before. I loved how the acidity of the watermelon cut through the fattiness of the mortadella and the richness of the fava beans. Well, that watermelon rind is long gone from the recipe, but rhubarb steps in without missing a beat. This is the perfect salad for a buffet since it thrives at room temperature and holds up well. It can also be made ahead, but do not add the vinaigrette until you're ready to serve, as the acid will turn the fava beans brown.

Serves 6 to 8 as an appetizer

2 rhubarb stalks, sliced ¼ inch thick (about ¾ cup)

½ cup plus 2 tablespoons white wine vinegar

Kosher salt

1 cup shelled fresh fava beans (see Notes)

Grated zest and juice of ½ blood orange (see Notes)

¼ cup olive oil

Freshly ground black pepper

1½ to 2 pounds mortadella (see Notes), cut into ¾-inch chunks

4 celery stalks, cut into ¼-inch slices (about 2 cups)

¼ cup Peppadew peppers, drained and chopped

¼ cup chopped celery leaves

¼ cup chopped fresh parsley

1 tablespoon crushed Calabrian chile pepper (optional)

In a bowl, combine the rhubarb and ½ cup of the vinegar. Season with salt. Let sit for 30 minutes to make a quick pickle, then drain (reserve the vinegar for another use).

Set up a bowl with equal parts water and ice and have nearby. Bring a medium pot of salted water to a boil for blanching the fava beans.

(recipe continues)

Blanch the fava beans in the boiling water for 3 to 4 minutes, until tender with no crunch. Drain and place in the ice bath. Drain and peel the beans by gently squeezing them between your fingers until they pop out of their skins. Set the favas in a bowl.

To make the vinaigrette, in a bowl, whisk together the blood orange zest and juice, olive oil, and remaining 2 tablespoons vinegar. Season generously with salt and black pepper.

In a serving bowl, toss together the mortadella, celery, quick-pickled rhubarb, Peppadew peppers, fava beans, celery leaves, parsley, and Calabrian chile (if you want to give the salad a little heat). Season with salt and black pepper. Add the vinaigrette, toss everything together, and serve at room temperature.

Notes:

- If you don't have fava beans, you can use snap peas that have been quickly blanched and then thinly sliced.

- If you can't find a blood orange, any orange will work.

- My favorite mortadella has pistachios in it. If you can't find this, add ½ cup pistachios to the mix.

- Ask your butcher for two ¾-inch slices of mortadella that are about 1 pound each, then cut the slices into cubes.

Green Shakshuka

In a traditional shakshuka, the eggs are nestled and poached in a mixture of spiced tomatoes, peppers, and onions. In this spring version, I go green instead of red, substituting a puree made of fresh blanched peas for the tomatoes. It's not only delicious but a wonderful way to incorporate fresh spring vegetables into your morning.

Serves 4

Kosher salt

1 bunch medium asparagus, ends trimmed, cut into 2-inch pieces

1 cup sugar snap peas, sliced

1 cup shelled fresh fava beans

1 cup shelled fresh English peas

1 cup vegetable stock or chicken broth

3 tablespoons unsalted butter

4 large eggs

Freshly ground black pepper

1 cup chopped pea tendrils

1 tablespoon extra-virgin olive oil

1 avocado, sliced

1 tablespoon chili crisp

Crusty bread, for serving

Preheat the oven to 350°F.

Set up a bowl with equal parts water and ice and have nearby. Bring a large pot of salted water to a boil for blanching the vegetables.

Add the asparagus to the boiling water and blanch for 1 to 2 minutes. Remove from the boiling water and immediately plunge into the bath. Scoop the asparagus out of the ice bath and set aside. Repeat the blanching process with the sugar snap peas and fava beans (the favas must then be peeled; squeeze to pop them out of their skins). Each vegetable should be blanched separately, but you can use the same boiling water and ice bath.

Add the English peas to the boiling water and cook for 1 minute. Scoop them out of the boiling water and transfer to a blender along with the vegetable stock (or blanching water). Add the butter and blend together until you have a smooth pea puree. Season with salt.

Pour the pea puree into a large ovenproof skillet, set the pan over low heat, and bring to a simmer. Gently crack the eggs into the pea puree, spacing them 2 inches apart or so. Nestle the blanched vegetables around the eggs and season with salt and pepper.

Transfer the pan to the oven and bake until the eggs are set, 8 to 10 minutes.

Remove the pan from the oven. Dress the shakshuka with the pea tendrils and a drizzle of olive oil. Top with the avocado and chili crisp and serve with crusty bread alongside.

Spring Vegetable Stew

A vignarola is a spring vegetable stew from Rome featuring artichokes, guanciale, spring onions, fava beans, and peas—basically, all that is bountiful in the spring in one dish. It's a simple preparation that allows the flavors of the season to shine through. It's perfect, or nearly. My only tweak to the classic recipe is to blanch the vegetables separately so they maintain their vibrant color, and then blanch the guanciale itself before pan-frying it, so that some of its fat is removed. The result is a brightly flavored, brightly colored taste of spring.

Serves 4 as a side or starter/makes 4½ cups

2 ounces guanciale, cut into ¼-inch dice

¼ cup extra-virgin olive oil

1 spring garlic stalk (see Note), white and light-green parts only, sliced

Kosher salt and freshly ground black pepper

1 bunch large asparagus, tops only (about 1 cup)

½ cup sugar snap peas, sliced on the bias

½ cup shelled fresh English peas

½ cup shelled fresh fava beans

½ recipe Braised Artichokes (page 157), with 1 cup of the liquid

4 cups packed spinach

¼ cup chopped fresh parsley

In a small pot, combine the guanciale with cold water to cover. Bring to a boil over medium heat. Once boiling, remove the guanciale to a plate and discard the water.

In a large sauté pan, warm the olive oil over low heat. Add the guanciale and cook until the fat turns translucent but not crispy, about 3 minutes. Stir in the garlic, season with salt and pepper, and cook, stirring occasionally, until the garlic is fragrant and the guanciale is just beginning to crisp around the edges, 4 to 5 minutes.

Set up a bowl with equal parts water and ice and have nearby. Bring a large pot of salted water to a boil for blanching the vegetables.

(recipe continues)

Add the asparagus to the boiling water and blanch for 1 to 2 minutes. Remove from the boiling water and immediately plunge it into the ice bath. Remove from the ice bath (and refresh the ice bath if needed) and set aside. Repeat the blanching and cold-shocking process with the sugar snaps, English peas, and favas (the favas will take 3 to 4 minutes and then must be peeled); you want to blanch each veg separately.

Add the braised artichokes, ½ to 1 cup of their liquid, and the spinach to the pan with the guanciale and garlic. (It should not be soupy.) Stir to combine. Increase the heat to medium. Slowly add all the blanched vegetables. Gently mix together and simmer until the vegetables are still bright but tender, 3 to 5 minutes. Season with salt and pepper. Add the parsley and serve.

Note: If you don't have spring garlic, you can use regular garlic instead.

Braised Artichokes

Makes about 2 cups

Juice of 1 lemon
8 small artichokes (about
    1 pound total)
½ cup extra-virgin olive oil
2 spring garlic stalks, white and
    light-green parts only, thinly
    sliced

Kosher salt
½ cup white wine
Freshly ground black pepper
½ cup chicken stock

In a large bowl, combine the lemon juice and 2 quarts water.

Trim each artichoke, removing the stem and outer green leaves. Use a serrated knife to trim off the top third of each artichoke and then cut each artichoke in half lengthwise. Add the trimmed artichokes to the lemon water as you work and keep them there until ready to use.

In a large sauté pan, heat the olive oil over medium-low heat. Drain the artichokes and add to the pan along with the spring garlic and a pinch of salt. Sweat the vegetables briefly, 2 to 3 minutes. Add the white wine and season with salt and pepper. Add the chicken stock and bring to a simmer. Slowly cook everything together, swirling the pan occasionally, until the artichokes are tender but not browned, 20 to 25 minutes.

Use immediately or store the braised artichokes in an airtight container in the fridge for up to 1 week.

Pasta with Spring Vegetables

When the garden gives you vegetables, it's best not to stand in the way. That's the idea behind this simple pasta, which is less a recipe and more an idea. Find your own ratios, substitute your own vegetables. (If you can't find spring garlic, for instance, use scallions. If you have ramps, for God's sake, use them!) Just make sure you have more pasta than peas. It is, after all, pasta with spring vegetables, not spring vegetables with pasta.

Serves 4

Kosher salt
1 pound pasta (any shape will do)
2 cups shelled fresh English peas
2 spring garlic stalks, white and
    light-green parts only, thinly
    sliced
Freshly ground black pepper

¼ cup extra-virgin olive oil
4 tablespoons unsalted butter
1 cup chopped pea tendrils
¼ cup chopped fresh mint
½ cup freshly grated pecorino
    cheese
½ cup ricotta cheese

Bring a large pot of salted water to a boil over high heat for the pasta.

Add the pasta and cook according to the package directions. About 2 minutes before cook time ends, add the peas and garlic to the water and allow them to cook with the pasta until the pasta is al dente.

Reserving 1 cup of the pasta water, drain the pasta and vegetables and return to the pot over medium heat. Season heavily with pepper. Add the olive oil and butter and mix until combined. Add some of the reserved pasta water, a little at a time, to achieve a saucy consistency. Turn off the heat and add the pea tendrils and mint. Add half of the pecorino, more salt and pepper, and mix everything together.

Portion the pasta into bowls and top each with 2 tablespoons ricotta. At the table, pass the remaining pecorino, salt, and pepper.

Southeast Asian–ish Curried Mussels

I love Southeast Asian food, though it doesn't fit into any restaurant that I currently have. But I love cooking it at home, where the crowd isn't so hard to please; no one there expects me to be perfect or a dish to be authentic. With these bold flavors—a perfectly balanced arrangement of heat, herbs, and acid—it's difficult not to want to eat these mussels all the time.

Serves 4

3 tablespoons extra-virgin olive oil

½ red onion, sliced

1 leek, green tops discarded, whites sliced into half-moons

Kosher salt

1 garlic clove, sliced

1 lemongrass stalk, trimmed and finely chopped

1-inch knob fresh ginger, peeled and cut into matchsticks

½ jalapeño, sliced

1 tablespoon curry powder

½ teaspoon fennel seeds

½ teaspoon cardamom seeds, lightly crushed

½ teaspoon coriander seeds, lightly crushed

2 pounds mussels, scrubbed and cleaned (see page 245)

One 13.5-ounce can coconut milk

Freshly ground black pepper

1 cup fresh Thai basil leaves, roughly chopped

1 cup fresh cilantro leaves, roughly chopped

Juice of 1 lime

Crusty baguette, for serving

In a large heavy-bottomed pot, warm the olive oil over medium heat. Add the onion and leek to the pot. Stir gently and season with salt. Cook until softened, 3 to 5 minutes. Add the garlic, lemongrass, ginger, and jalapeño and stir to combine. Mix in the curry powder and the fennel, cardamom, and coriander seeds and cook until fragrant, about 30 seconds.

(recipe continues)

Add the mussels and coconut milk to the pot. Season with salt and pepper and cover the pot with a tight-fitting lid. Let the mussels simmer over low heat, 8 to 10 minutes, until all the mussels have opened. Shake the pot every now and then to agitate the mussels. Discard any mussels that don't open.

Once the mussels are opened and cooked, add the basil and cilantro. Drizzle with lime juice and serve with a crusty baguette.

Sea Bass with Braised Artichokes, Asparagus, and Rhubarb

This gather-from-the-garden-and-go dinner comes together rather quickly. It's a one-pan preparation that allows all the flavors of the vegetables to commingle, while the braising liquid becomes a light subtle broth served alongside the sea bass.

Serves 4

Kosher salt

1 bunch medium asparagus, ends trimmed, cut in half lengthwise

4 skin-on black sea bass fillets (3 ounces each) or any firm white fish, such as rockfish or snapper

Freshly ground black pepper

2 tablespoons extra-virgin olive oil

½ recipe Braised Artichokes (page 157)

1 stalk rhubarb, cut into ¼-inch pieces

1 cup pea tendrils

Set up a bowl with equal parts water and ice and have nearby. Bring a large pot of salted water to a boil for blanching the asparagus.

Add the asparagus to the boiling water and blanch for 1 to 2 minutes. Remove from the boiling water and immediately plunge into the ice bath. Drain and set aside.

Rinse the sea bass fillets under cold water, pat dry, and season with salt and pepper on both sides.

In a large skillet, heat the olive oil over medium heat. When the oil is hot, add the fillets skin-side down and sear until crispy, 3 to 4 minutes. Transfer the seared fish, skin-side up, to a plate.

Pour the fat out of the skillet and wipe the skillet clean. Add the braised artichokes and their liquid and set over medium-low heat. Add the rhubarb and asparagus and season with salt and pepper. Nestle in the fish, skin-side up. There should be enough braising liquid to come just to the top of the fish, not covering it. (You can add a little additional chicken stock or water if needed.) Cook until the fish flakes easily, 4 to 5 minutes.

Transfer the fish to plates. Spoon the broth and vegetables around the fish. Season with salt and pepper, top with pea tendrils, and serve.

Marinated Roasted Swordfish with Meyer Lemons and Rosemary

Twenty years ago, I never would have shared a recipe for swordfish. By the late 1990s, swordfish was in decline. Between 1960 and 1996 the swordfish population had been reduced by 65 percent and the size of the fish caught grew smaller and smaller. In the late '90s, a campaign called "Give Swordfish a Break," organized by chefs, helped convince the United States government to put measures in place to conserve the fish. Thankfully, due to sustainable fishing practices and dedicated conservationists, the swordfish population has returned to health and the fish has returned to menus. That's great news since there are few fish that can rival the robust meatiness of swordfish. In this recipe I use a marinating technique that I learned at the Quilted Giraffe. By separating the fish from the marinade with cheesecloth, you get all the flavors but don't have to worry about removing any bits of garlic or shallot that might burn. This recipe is quick to make, but you'll need some forethought to allow time for it to marinate.

Serves 4

MARINATED SWORDFISH
¼ cup extra-virgin olive oil
2 garlic cloves, minced
2 sprigs fresh rosemary
1 shallot, minced
4 swordfish steaks (6 to 8 ounces each)

TO FINISH
2 lemons, cut into thick rounds
2 sprigs fresh rosemary
4 tablespoons extra-virgin olive oil
Kosher salt

Marinate the swordfish: In a small bowl, mix together the olive oil, garlic, rosemary, and shallot. Pour the marinade into a shallow baking dish to cover the bottom. Cover with a single layer of cheesecloth and place the swordfish steaks on top of the cheesecloth. Cover with plastic wrap and place in the fridge to marinate for 24 hours.

(recipe continues)

167

To finish: Preheat a grill or large grill pan over medium-high heat.

In a bowl, toss the lemon rounds and rosemary sprigs with 2 tablespoons of the olive oil and season with salt. Grill, turning occasionally, until browned, 8 to 10 minutes. Remove the lemons and rosemary to a plate.

Remove the swordfish from the marinade. Season the swordfish steaks on both sides with salt and drizzle with the remaining 2 tablespoons olive oil.

Grill the fish, flipping once, until golden brown and the internal temperature reads 130° to 140°F, 3 to 4 minutes per side.

Transfer to a platter and serve with the grilled lemons and rosemary.

Spring Chicken Meatballs

Meatballs have the reputation of being heavy and hearty. Some are (see Sunday Gravy with Meatballs and Braciole, page 123). But they don't have to be. This version is a lovely light lunch or dinner, as healthy as it is tasty. A complete springtime meal, it uses the bounty of green vegetables—I use peas, asparagus, and spinach; you can use whatever you have—and herbaceous ground chicken meatballs.

Makes 16 meatballs/serves 4

Kosher salt
1 pound ground chicken
Freshly ground black pepper
1 tablespoon freshly grated Parmesan cheese, plus more for serving
1 large egg, whisked
¼ cup chopped fresh parsley
½ teaspoon coriander seeds, crushed
½ teaspoon fennel seeds, crushed
4 tablespoons extra-virgin olive oil, plus more as needed and for drizzling

½ cup plus 1 tablespoon chicken stock, plus more if needed
1 bunch asparagus, ends trimmed, cut into 2-inch pieces (about 1 cup)
1 cup shelled fresh English peas
2 spring onions, white and light-green parts only, thinly sliced
1 cup packed spinach
2 tablespoons chopped fresh dill
Grated zest of 1 lemon

Bring a large pot of salted water to a boil for blanching the vegetables.

Meanwhile, in a bowl, season the chicken generously with salt and pepper. Add the Parmesan and egg and mix everything together. Add the parsley, coriander seeds, and fennel seeds and mix again.

Divide the mixture into 16 equal portions and form into 1-inch balls. The mixture will be sticky, so it's important to roll the meatballs with wet hands. You can place the meatballs on a sheet of parchment as you roll them.

(recipe continues)

In a heavy-bottomed pan, heat 2 tablespoons of the olive oil over medium-low heat. When the oil is hot, add the meatballs and brown them on all sides, 5 to 7 minutes total. You can do this in batches, depending on your pan size, adding more oil as needed.

If browning in batches, return all the meatballs to the pan. Pour in the chicken stock, adding more if needed so the broth comes about halfway up the meatballs. Bring to a simmer, then reduce the heat to low, cover, and poach the meatballs until cooked through, about 5 minutes.

Meanwhile, set up a large bowl with equal parts water and ice and have near the stove. Add the asparagus to the pot of salted boiling water and blanch for 1 to 2 minutes. Quickly remove the asparagus and drop into the ice bath to stop the cooking. Drain well. Don't let the asparagus sit in the cold water too long; remove it to a plate.

Blanch the peas in the same way as the asparagus. Drain well.

In a large sauté pan, heat the remaining 2 tablespoons oil over medium-low heat. Add the spring onions and a pinch of salt and let them sweat until just lightly translucent, about 2 minutes. Add the blanched and drained asparagus and English peas. Stir to combine. Pour in 1 tablespoon of chicken stock and add the spinach. Season with salt and pepper. Let cook for 1 to 2 minutes, until the spinach has just wilted.

Add the vegetables to the pan with the meatballs and mix everything together gently.

To serve, plate the meatballs and vegetables and top with fresh dill, some grated Parmesan, lemon zest, a bit more olive oil, salt, and pepper.

Grilled Quail with Salsa Verde

Slightly gamy and very tender, quail is an underrated bird. Home cooks often seem intimidated by it, as if the work-to-meat ratio isn't worth the trouble. But already boned-out quail, such as you can get through D'Artagnan or other suppliers, is as easy as chicken to cook and has a charm all its own. This recipe works well on the stovetop but even better on a wood grill. (A good middle ground is a grill pan on the stove.) Though I'm generally opposed to using ripping high heat, quail is small enough that it's called for here and even necessary to crisp the birds.

As for the salsa verde, I'm not a big sauce guy at home, but this one is so versatile and keeps so well, it's one of my staples. Feel free to make it ahead of time, but if you do, don't add the vinegar until the last minute or the acid will turn the sauce brown.

Serve with Green Farro (page 177) alongside.

Serves 4

QUAIL
4 semi-boneless quail
Kosher salt and freshly ground
  black pepper
¼ cup extra-virgin olive oil
3 garlic cloves, smashed
3 sprigs fresh rosemary

1 teaspoon chili crisp, or to taste,
  or ½ teaspoon red pepper
  flakes
Kosher salt and freshly ground
  black pepper
1 tablespoon red wine vinegar
1 tablespoon capers

SALSA VERDE
2 cups chopped fresh parsley
1 cup extra-virgin olive oil
1 shallot, finely diced

TO FINISH
2 tablespoons extra-virgin
  olive oil

Prepare the quail: Place the quail in a shallow bowl. Season generously with salt and pepper. Cover it with the olive oil, garlic, and rosemary. Turn to coat and allow to marinate for 15 to 30 minutes.

(recipe continues)

Meanwhile, make the salsa verde: In a bowl, mix together the parsley, olive oil, shallot, and chili crisp. Season with salt and pepper and mix again. Add the vinegar and capers. Check and adjust the seasoning.

To finish: Place a grill pan or large heavy skillet over medium heat and pour in the olive oil. Add the quail (do this in batches as necessary) and cook until browned and firm to the touch, about 5 minutes per side.

Serve the quail alongside the salsa verde.

Storage: Store the salsa verde in an airtight container for up to 3 days in the fridge. If making in advance, do not add the vinegar and capers until ready to serve.

Green Farro

Farro verde, or green farro, is harvested during a brief window early in its growing season, while the farro is still unripe. The result is a chewy and lightly smoky flavor that I love. I source my farro from Anson Mills, out of Columbia, South Carolina. Green farro is great as a side dish for any roasted meat. I frequently make it with the Grilled Quail with Salsa Verde (page 173).

Serves 4 as a starter or side

2 tablespoons extra-virgin
   olive oil
1 carrot, chopped
1 celery stalk, chopped
1 leek, white part only, chopped
Kosher salt

1½ cups green farro
2 to 3 cups chicken stock or
   water
Freshly ground black pepper
2 sprigs fresh thyme

In a medium saucepan, heat the olive oil over medium-low heat. Add the carrot, celery, leek, and a pinch of salt. Sweat the vegetables, stirring occasionally, until just translucent, 5 to 7 minutes.

Add the farro and enough stock or water to just cover the farro by ½ inch. Season with salt and pepper and add the thyme. Cover and cook until the farro is tender, 30 to 40 minutes.

Remove from the heat, fluff the farro with a fork, and serve.

Porchetta with Spring Garlic, Fennel, and Potatoes

Porchetta is rolled pork belly. It's going to be fatty . . . so fatty it should be served with a side of Lipitor. So don't complain that it's fatty. That's also why it's delicious. Some porchetta is made skin-on and crisped by drizzling hot oil over the skin so it puffs up like a chicharrón. That is incredibly difficult to achieve at home. When I make porchetta, I get my pork belly with the skin removed and then let it rest in the fridge overnight, so the surface dries out a bit (and the herbs rubbed inside infuse it). The result is as impressive as it is simple to make.

Serves 8 to 10

5 pounds skinless pork belly
½ cup extra-virgin olive oil
5 garlic cloves, minced
Leaves from 2 sprigs fresh rosemary, roughly chopped, plus 3 or 4 whole rosemary sprigs
2 tablespoons fennel seeds, crushed
Grated zest of 1 orange

Kosher salt and freshly ground black pepper
1 pound small Yukon Gold potatoes, cut into ¼-inch rounds
4 spring garlic stems, white bulbs only, halved lengthwise
1 large fennel bulb, cut into eighths

Lay the pork belly flat on a work surface and use a small knife to create shallow crosshatching on the meaty side of the pork (the nonfat side).

In a small bowl, mix together the olive oil, garlic, rosemary leaves, fennel seeds, and orange zest. Season the pork belly generously with salt and pepper. Spread the oil and herb mixture all over the inside of the pork belly, massaging it into the crosshatches.

(recipe continues)

Starting from a short side, very tightly roll the pork belly into a log shape. Use butcher's twine to tie the pork; space the ties 1 to 2 inches apart. Season the outside of the pork generously with salt. You can cook it at this point but it's ideal to allow the pork to sit overnight uncovered in the fridge (place it on a sheet pan).

Remove the pork belly from the fridge 1 hour to 1 hour 30 minutes in advance of cooking to allow it to come to room temperature.

When you're ready to cook, preheat the oven to 325°F.

Place the porchetta in a large roasting pan and roast until the fat has softened and the internal temperature of the pork registers about 160°F, about 3 hours.

Remove the pork from the oven and scatter the potatoes, spring garlic, fresh fennel, and rosemary sprigs around it. Season the vegetables lightly with salt and pepper.

Return the pan to the oven and roast until the veggies are cooked through, 45 minutes to 1 hour.

Increase the oven temperature to 400°F and cook the pork for an additional 15 minutes to crisp the pork and get the vegetables golden.

Remove the porchetta from the oven and let rest for about 15 minutes before cutting. Serve slices of porchetta with the roasted vegetables.

Rib Eye with Portobello Mushrooms and Salsa Verde

What's there to say that isn't clear from a steak recipe? A rib eye is primal and its pleasures self-evident. Here I serve it with some scallions, onions, and mushrooms, all cooked—serially—in the same pan so that they benefit from the accumulated juices given off by the steak.

Serves 3 or 4

1½- to 2-pound bone-in rib eye
(about 1½ inches thick)
Kosher salt
2 tablespoons extra-virgin
olive oil

4 portobello mushrooms, left
whole
2 red onions, cut into rounds
1 bunch scallions, trimmed and
left whole
Salsa Verde (page 173)

Remove the rib eye from the refrigerator 30 to 60 minutes in advance of cooking to allow it to come to room temperature.

Preheat the oven to 450°F.

Season the rib eye liberally with salt on both sides.

In a large ovenproof skillet, warm the olive oil over medium heat until shimmering. Add the steak and sear it for 3 to 4 minutes per side. Transfer the steak to the oven to finish cooking—you can insert a thermometer now; you want the internal temperature to reach 130°F for medium-rare or 135°F for medium.

When the steak reaches the desired temperature, carefully remove it from the oven, transfer the steak to a cutting board, and allow to rest.

Meanwhile, return the pan to medium heat. Working in batches so you don't crowd the pan, add the portobello mushrooms and season with salt. Cook the mushrooms, pressing down on them with a spatula to ensure a good sear, until tender, 3 to 5 minutes per side. Remove the mushrooms to a cutting board, slice them, and transfer to a large bowl along with any accumulated juices.

Place the onions in the same pan and cook over medium heat, flipping once, until just soft and browned, 5 to 7 minutes. Transfer the onions to the bowl with the mushrooms.

Add the scallions to the pan and cook until just soft, 3 to 4 minutes. Add them to the bowl with the mushrooms and onions and mix all the vegetables together.

Just before slicing, return the steak to a hot oven to warm it up for a few minutes. Once warm, slice the steak and pour any accumulated juices over the top. Serve the steak with grilled vegetables over the top and the salsa verde alongside.

7

Soul Food

BACK IN NEW YORK, I now had a clear idea of my next move. I'd heard about a chef named Thomas Keller who was opening a restaurant called Rakel in West SoHo. (The name was a portmanteau of his name and the name of his partner, Serge Raoul.) Thomas was from Florida and had worked in Rhode Island and the Hudson Valley before making his way around New York and Paris. He had developed a reputation as someone to watch; Rakel had buzz even before it opened. I paid Thomas a visit and we talked. He struck me as driven and cerebral, almost monklike in his devotion to craft. Thomas offered me a job on the line, and I took it.

Working with Thomas was challenging but worth it. He ran a tight ship. Cooks could converse, but it had better be about the food. Every moment was suffused with a sense of urgency and purpose. What made it tolerable was that Thomas followed his own rules, drove himself harder than anyone, and was refreshingly experimental, which kept me on my toes and endlessly interested. When the sous-chef left after a few months, Thomas gave me the job. As a chef,

Thomas was rigorous and exacting, but if he trusted you, he could be generous, too. If a VIP walked in, he'd say across the stove, "Tom, make something special," and I would wing it. No idea was too far out or over the top. One night I suggested we roast an entire double lobe of foie gras for a party of ten, something I'd never attempted or even seen (clearly, I had left Gascony, but it hadn't left me). "It better work," Thomas told me, which sounded like permission. It came out great. I loved the spirit of collaboration he encouraged, even as he pushed me to execute at the highest possible level.

This was some of the cleanest, most focused food I'd ever made, and while we certainly caught the attention of foodies and fellow chefs, the restaurant never fully caught on. It could have been the location—a stretch of no-man's-land above Tribeca. It could have been a disconnect between the sophistication of the food—roast lobster with beet syrup, or cappuccino of foie gras—and the downtown vibe, which in 1987 was still more Andy Warhol than André Soltner. The identity crisis extended inside as well: Half of the space was a bar, clubby and fun; Thomas's half was a sober, serious restaurant. Though we earned a glowing two-star review from Bryan Miller at the *New York Times*, Rakel wasn't financially successful. I could see that it wore heavily on Thomas, the frustration of doing great work and not having it land as it deserved to. We all felt it. Not once, though, did Thomas consider lowering his standards or revisiting the concept. Rakel was his vision, and he was totally committed to seeing it through.

I was glad to be at Rakel, but I wouldn't have called it a happy place. It ran on tension. Money woes meant we were chronically understaffed, each of us responsible for a mountain of intricate mise en place every day, which we'd set to with an anxious eye on the clock as service loomed. For months we were short an entremetier, the cook responsible for the vegetables and apps on the meat side, and I took over that job along with my own. It was grueling, and the pressure was nearly unbearable at times. One of the dishes on my list was a rolled saddle of venison stuffed with mushroom duxelles, which we roasted wrapped in caul fat to keep the venison moist. Caul fat is the thin, lacelike membrane that surrounds the organs of pigs and cows, and before use it needs to be soaked well in ice water to clean it up and remove its impurities. I was gearing up for service one night, the usual impossible race against time. I'd soaked the caul fat in cold water the night before, changing out the bath twice. As I wrung out the fat, Thomas walked by, glanced at it, and told me to soak the entire thing again. It was minutes before service, and I was already in the weeds, but I placed it back in the ice water, then started getting sauces set up for service while it soaked. As the doors to the restaurant were opening, I pulled the caul fat from the water, wringing it out, so I could get the venison wrapped and ready before orders started coming in. The fat wasn't as white as it could have been, but at this point, as sous-chef, I figured I had three choices: use the caul fat as it was, roast the venison without caul fat, or 86 the dish. I decided to continue wrapping, knowing most of it would melt away from the high heat of the roast. Thomas approached my station again and angrily grabbed the mass of caul fat, throwing it back into the bucket, shouting "I told you to soak this!" Heads around the kitchen popped up to watch.

I have a temper, which I knew better than to unleash in another man's kitchen. But the months of unrelenting stress and pressure were working on me, too. My better angels did not prevail. "You know what?" I said. "I quit." I took off my apron, walked out of the kitchen, and headed home. The next day Thomas and I talked. I told him it just wasn't working out for me. I understood that he needed to ride people, and that he rode himself harder than anyone. But it was no longer a great fit. In part, this was me coming to a realization about myself: I chafed under someone else's rules, whether they made sense or not. I was feeling the itch to go out on my own and be my own boss. Thomas understood—he'd been there himself. We parted friends, which we are to this day.

As usual, I'd acted first and dealt with the consequences later. As I plotted my next move, I got a frantic call from my old friend Jerry. He had moved back home to Virginia to open a restaurant complex called The Max in Portsmouth and asked me to come and help. It was a massive undertaking: a fine-dining restaurant, a casual café, a

Me with Drew Nieporent in 1988

club with its own full menu, and a series of banquet rooms for weddings and private events. The owner, Charlie Sears, insisted he open for breakfast, lunch, and dinner—in all of them—from day one. I planned on helping for a couple of weeks and ended up staying for nine months.

On a trip home from Virginia, I was invited to the christening of Ariane Daguin's daughter. The room was thick with restaurant folk, including a young Drew Nieporent, who had newly opened Montrachet, and a chef from Chatham, New Jersey, named Dennis Foy, whom I knew from my days cooking in New Jersey. Dennis was on the cusp of opening a restaurant in Midtown named Mondrian and was hiring. George Faison, Ariane's partner in D'Artagnan, pointed at me and said, "If you need someone to run the restaurant, pick him." A few weeks later, Dennis flew down to Virginia Beach to make me a formal offer.

It was tempting, but I declined. I had been itching to get back to France, especially since my aborted *stage* in Paris. I had recently read an article by Paula Wolfert in the *New York Times* about the French chef Michel Bras, at Lou Mazuc, a restaurant in the Massif Central, a craggy highland in south-central France. Bras approached vegetables and herbs with a botanist's eye, centering the dish around their natural colors and flavors in a way that I found exciting. He took André Daguin's naturalism a step further—his food seemed almost to tumble onto the plate, eschewing the studied symmetry typical of French cuisine. Through Ariane, I offered myself up for a *stage*, and an invitation followed. I was on my way to France.

But fate had something else in store for me. My parents came to visit me in Virginia, and my father told me he hadn't been feeling well. In typical fashion he downplayed it, but when they got home, my mother insisted he go in for a full medical workup. Afterward, the doctors sat them down for the news nobody wants: My father had stage IV lung cancer, incurable and untreatable. It wasn't surprising; after all, he'd been a two-pack-a-day smoker since the age of twelve. But he was only fifty-two, his life only partly lived. The doctors gave him a few months at best. I immediately canceled my *stage* and called up Dennis to see if the job at Mondrian was still available. It was.

Mondrian was opening in the former Playboy Club on East 59th Street. Dennis's main backer was an astute and likable banker from Morgan Stanley named Bob Scott. He and four other Morgan Stanley guys wanted a place where they would eat well and always get a table. Money was no object and the design was unapologetically luxe: cherrywood on the walls, elegant flowers refreshed daily, chairs of buttery leather. Dennis Foy was a colorful character. He was a raconteur and partyer who claimed to have been a Green Beret in Vietnam. While not quite on the vanguard of American cuisine, like Thomas Keller or Barry Wine, he was respected nevertheless. If I was honest with myself, I didn't love his food; to me it felt fussy and predictable. Nor was I a fan of his style: When he didn't like something, he'd get right in our faces to shout, like a drill sergeant. Despite this, Dennis was a generous and thoughtful boss. He lent me his car when mine was in the shop. If we finished late, he'd give me keys to an apartment in the city where I could crash. He encouraged me to put a couple of my own dishes on the menu.

In the primordial days before social media, new restaurants got buzz through gatekeepers, a group of influential writers, foodies, and cookbook authors whose opinions often guided public consensus. A well-known example is Tim Zagat, whose (snail mail) newsletter about the restaurants he enjoyed eventually became the Zagat guide. Others were Peter Kump, a contemporary of James Beard, who founded an eponymous cooking school that eventually became the Institute of Culinary Education; Sheila Lukins, the author of *The Silver Palate Cookbook*; and Barbara Kafka, a celebrated restaurant consultant who had helped open Windows on the World with Joe Baum. After a meal at Mondrian, Barbara invited Dennis to lunch to share her views with him in private. He came back to the kitchen ashen and subdued. It was clear that Barbara hadn't liked the food, and the consequences, once her views became known, would be dire. I was bereft right along with him—after all the hard work we'd put in, the thought of Mondrian bombing right out of the gate was devastating. "Was there anything she liked?" I asked. Dennis held up the menu. "This. And this," he answered, pointing to my two dishes. He flung the menu down and went to the bar.

I barely had the bandwidth to process all this. For the first time since I was fifteen, my work wasn't my main concern. As soon as my shift was done, I'd hightail it back to Elizabeth to be with my father. Where his silences had once unnerved me, now they felt comfortable. I'd sit quietly with him hooked up to his IV, only the TV and his fits of guttural coughing between us. My brothers and mother did the same. We took comfort just being in the room with him. My father's illness had pulled us together.

My dad's decline was rapid. A month after diagnosis, he was home and in hospice care. Dad faced death as stoically as he had everything else life had thrown at him. My mother worked hard to keep him comfortable, but he grew testy. One of his few remaining pleasures, he insisted, was smoking—could someone please get him a goddamn cigarette? When no one would, he dragged himself out of their second-story apartment, down the stairs, and across the street to buy a pack of smokes. The whole family was up in arms about it, but he couldn't care less. Secretly I agreed with him. Why should we deny him this last pleasure? He was going either way.

My father died just after Thanksgiving. I took three weeks off from Mondrian and surrounded myself with family and friends. I could hardly have done otherwise; my father was the first of my parents' cohort to go, and their apartment was filled with friends and relatives who stayed late into the night sharing stories about him. His wake was like no other I had ever attended—an uninterrupted stream of well-wishers from early morning until closing, including everyone he'd ever worked with, his childhood friends from the block, our friends from the Gran Centurions, an endless array of cousins. On the day of his funeral, Elizabeth police closed off the streets to traffic and provided an escort—the procession was two miles long. I felt grief at my father's passing, but also a sense of peace. Though we hadn't talked much, as always, there had been something easy and loving in the air between us over those last few months; no need for words.

When I returned to Mondrian, Dennis handed control of the kitchen to me, giving me free rein over the menu. I immediately filled it with new ideas along with dishes I had been working on for years. Most nights Dennis entertained an audience at the bar, while I held it down behind the swinging doors. Soon we started to get noticed. To my excitement, *New York* magazine called to say they would be featuring one of my dishes, a pureed oyster stew garnished with fried oysters and black truffle, in an upcoming issue. When the issue came out, I opened it excitedly. There was a beautiful picture of the dish, and over it, the title read: "Dennis Foy's Fried Oyster Stew." My heart sank. I'm not sure what I was expecting—after all, it isn't uncommon for chefs to get credit for the work of the cooks they are teaching—but at that moment something clicked for me. I hadn't created the dish under Dennis's tutelage; it developed in an organic process made up of years of my own learnings and the philosophies I had absorbed from my real teachers, and not getting the credit stung. I was also different than I had been mere weeks before. My father's passing had reminded me just how short and precious life is. I couldn't waste any more time standing still. I had my own ideas to pursue, and they demanded that I keep learning and growing. It was time to go back to France.

I gave Dennis my notice and called Ariane, who quickly plugged in the necessary wires, and I was on my way. The plan was to work for three months with Michel Bras and then for three months with the great Alain Ducasse in Biarritz.

I spent the summer of 1989 in a town called Laguiole, in the starkly beautiful highlands of south-central France where Michel Bras ran the kitchen of his parents' restaurant, Lou Mazuc. Michel had grown up here, and he was a born naturalist, deeply in tune with the growing cycles and fauna of his surroundings. He was hyperlocal before that was a thing: From the stream, he drew trout; from the farms, lambs and calves. He was a long-distance runner who had an intimacy with the terrain around him that informed his foraging for mushrooms, nuts, and wild herbs. In her review, Paula Wolfert wrote that Michel "raised peasant cooking to a new and extraordinary level," and it was true. His cooking had a distinct point of view, and I became an immediate devotee.

Bras's food was impeccable but not fancy. He was famous for his gargouillou, a dish of vegetables, lightly blanched, cooked in a beurre fondue, then scattered loosely but intentionally on the plate with borage flowers and nasturtium. The presentation—a bit "off" by design—excited me. It drew the eye to the individual vegetables in a fresh and inspiring way, while still unifying them as a coherent dish. I also loved how Michel would bake a piece of salmon in a low oven with steam just to the point that it would set up, then carefully lift off the skin and scrape off the fat before covering the fish with chives and laying it on the plate with a few broad beans and a reduction of Banyuls, a portlike wine from the Pyrenees. This dish epitomized Michel's approach to heat; he eschewed a hard sear on his food, not wanting the strong browned taste of a Maillard reaction to interfere with the intrinsic flavors of the ingredients.

Lou Mazuc was a family affair. Michel's wife, Ginette, ran the front of the house, and his mother, Angèle, made the nightly aligot, a side dish of pureed potato hand-beaten with earthy Tomme de Savoie, an alpine cheese. Michel and Ginette's son, Sébastien, was a baby, passed from hand to hand during family meal (today he's a great chef in his own right). What I loved most about Michel's food was that the ingredients told him what to do, not the other way around. It sounds corny, but Michel cooked from his soul. His food lacked even a whiff of pretension, while still rivaling the best in Paris, Switzerland, or New York. As I stood next to Michel at the pass, I could see how free he was. I knew that, if given the chance, I wanted to cook like this one day in my own kitchen—from the sweet spot where instinct, experience, and training meet.

And then, in the fall of 1989, I got a call from Bob Scott, the principal investor at Mondrian. When my father was dying, Bob had welcomed me into his home warmly, sensing I could use a break. This time, he was calling from New York with an ask, and it was urgent. Mondrian was failing. "Tom," he said, "Dennis is AWOL. I need you to come back and run the place." And so I did.

IT HAD BEEN ONLY THREE MONTHS since I'd left Mondrian, but it felt like a wholly different place when I returned. I realize now it was me who had changed. I arrived energized and inspired by what I'd learned in Laguiole, my mind buzzing with ideas. I immediately called my friend Kerry to see if he'd come on as sous-chef, and to my great fortune, he agreed. Kerry and I would lob ideas for dishes back and forth between us, sometimes building a concept together, other times spiraling off separately to improvise. We'd cook side by side, trying things out, tasting, tossing, starting again, switching something out, refining, then adding something from out of left field to see how it played. My vision of the menu gradually took form, borrowing from the best of what I had learned at Quilted and Rakel and Hôtel de France and Lou Mazuc. Each place I'd worked left its thumbprint on me; each place had a philosophy that whispered in my ear as I worked. I didn't have a name for the type of food I was making. I still don't.

What followed was the most purposeful and creative period I'd ever experienced. I'd get to the restaurant at 10 a.m. and stay until midnight or 1 a.m., seven days a week, but I don't recall feeling tired. I now keenly understood the intensity and single-mindedness Thomas had brought to every aspect of Rakel, that feeling that each choice—from wine list to music to service—should be an expression of the higher idea, of the gestalt. I tried to find ingredients like I'd seen in France, which meant forming relationships with farmers like

Guy Jones at Blooming Hill Farm, who had a subversive streak and was game to grow new and eccentric vegetables. I had snuck some crosnes—tiny spiral crucifers—back to the States with me and asked Guy to grow them. These were the early days of the Union Square Greenmarket, when no one stopped you from backing your car right up to the stalls to load up. The market was a marvel back then; farmers were in a new and deep symbiosis with chefs, willing to take risks with what they grew for those of us who sought them out. Urban greenmarkets became a lifeline for small farmers and eventually caught on with other consumers, foodies and general shoppers alike. Today they tend to stay in line with what they know will sell, at the expense of new and unusual ingredients. But back then there was a variety and weirdness to the produce you'd find there, and for chefs who were combing through the bins alongside me, like Michael Romano from Union Square Cafe and Peter Hoffman from Savoy, the place still felt like our secret.

Those gatekeepers that Dennis had courted started showing up at Mondrian. Sheila Lukins became a regular, as did David

Rosengarten and Josh Wesson, coauthors of the witty and influential newsletter *Wine & Food Companion*, who wrote enthusiastically about us. In October 1990, Bryan Miller, the reviewer for the *New York Times*, awarded us three stars. Life was suddenly dramatically different; I was a three-star chef in the heart of New York City, at the apex of American dining culture. Some of the impostor syndrome I had felt that summer at Yves Picot's home returned. But walking through the dining room, I'd see chefs I admired, like Jean-Jacques Rachou from La Côte Basque and Gérard Pangaud from Aurora, and restaurateurs like Ken Aretsky, Alan Stillman, and Danny Meyer enjoying my food. They'd come back repeatedly, as would my "fellow travelers" in New American cuisine, Jonathan Waxman and Larry Forgione. Thomas Keller showed up, and his pleasure at both my food and my success was apparent. The only thing that could have made this moment better was if my father had been alive to see it.

8

Gramercy Tavern

MONDRIAN WAS A HIT. The glowing *New York Times* review was soon followed by a fantastic writeup in *New York* magazine by Gael Greene, and I was named one of *Food & Wine* magazine's best new chefs at the 1991 Aspen Food & Wine Classic, an annual conclave of chefs, writers, restaurant industry people, and food lovers. In addition to Kerry Heffernan, Mondrian's kitchen was filled with talent like Bobby Schneider, Vincent Barcelona, and a young baker Kerry was dating named Amy Scherber, fresh off a *stage* in France, whom I hired to make our bread (she later went on to open Amy's Bread). As a team we clicked, moving together and apart under the storm of nightly orders like sprockets of a well-oiled gear. The pressure of a restaurant kitchen can forge a bond among cooks, one that reminds me of the bond shared among soldiers who have been to battle together. The work calls for a high level of cooperation and interdependence. Disasters are felt collectively. Split-second changes require a sort of group agility, and we achieved that, while also having fun, thanks to a pair of Chinese dishwashers who spoke almost no English but kept us

---

in stitches. (One of them called himself Mr. Party, and he was forever trying to fix Kerry up with his daughter.) Around the holidays they took all of us—me, sous-chefs, prep staff—to a place in Chinatown for dim sum that to this day is the best I've ever had. I was less wild about our front-of-house staff, a team of Croatian captains and waiters from the Dennis days who were possessed of an extraordinary knack for calculating guests' net worth from their watches and shoes and then treating them accordingly.

Most nights I was too busy to do laps of the dining room, but on occasion I would pop out to make guests feel welcome. Thanks to our Morgan Stanley backers, we became a favorite destination of Wall Streeters, the rock stars of the late '80s, and once Peter Buck—guitarist for R.E.M. and a real foodie—discovered us, some actual rock stars made their way through as well. Jean-Paul and Monique Picot—Yves's parents, as gracious as ever—came in frequently to cheer me on. Most heartening of all, we soon had a band of regulars, including Sheila Lukins and the great Jim Henson, creator of the Muppets (and a personal hero). It was a great feeling to see the dining room packed nightly. And yet there was a big problem: We were losing money. The lease for our space had been negotiated before I got there at the height of the market—just before the crash in October 1987—and it boiled down to bad math: There was no way we could afford the $35,000-a-month rent with an eighty-seat dining room, no matter how much people loved us.

I tried to renegotiate our lease with our landlord, the Hong Kong Bank, but they weren't interested. I gained a new appreciation for Thomas Keller's travails at Rakel. Doing excellent work may be its own reward, but Mondrian was a business, not performance art, and I hated ending each month in the red. Soon the old itch returned: the nagging back-of-the-brain urge to do better, forge forward, try something else. An idea was taking shape in my mind. At the 1992 Aspen Food & Wine Classic, I had been seated next to Danny Meyer. We'd known each other casually for years, but this was the first time we'd truly connected one-on-one, and I felt a synergy with him. Danny was famous for the warm hospitality he'd pioneered at

Union Square Cafe, an extension of his own sincerity and charm. At the time this was still rare in the starchy world of fine dining, and the service had become as much of a draw for Union Square's diners as the food. Maybe the solution to Mondrian's problem was to unyoke myself entirely from its onerous lease and start fresh with someone whose approach to service mirrored my approach to food—serious but unstuffy and accessible? I called Bob Scott and floated the idea of closing Mondrian and finding a new location with lower rent and more capacity. Would he back this new endeavor? Bob said he'd think it over.

Happily, there was something distracting me from Mondrian's financial woes. I had a new girlfriend, a Smith Barney banker named Kristen Johanson, who had approached me after dinner one night and asked me out. I'm a sucker for smart, confident women, so naturally I said yes. Her loft in Hell's Kitchen was an easy walk after service from Mondrian, and pretty soon I'd moved in my stuff and become enfolded in her world. Kristen had been an economics major at Williams College. Her friends were Ivy League types, engaged in the larger world, with white-collar jobs and perfect syntax. At first I'd hang back when I was with them, my old insecurity gnawing away. Was I too Jersey? Was I getting it right? But they were nice, fun people who didn't give a hoot where I'd come from or (not) gone to school. I had always been a voracious reader and an avid consumer of the news, and I was surprised to learn I could keep up with them, even with my crappy syntax. My deficits, as they were, were figments of my imagination.

Meanwhile, the math at Mondrian wasn't getting any better. I was sick of working so hard and not turning a profit. When I again floated the idea of shutting it down past Bob, this time he agreed with me. He also agreed to back a new venture, downtown, if we could find the right space and the right deal. And that was that. In July 1992 Mondrian's doors closed for good. Saying goodbye to our team was sad, but I nonetheless felt optimistic. I now knew I could do the work of creating a New York City restaurant that was my own and that people would show up. It's a great feeling to have people on your side, people who believe in you. I was buoyed by the idea that something even better lay ahead.

I had run into Danny Meyer again a few months earlier at the Aspen Food & Wine Classic and liked him just as much as I had the previous year. Right before we announced Mondrian's closing, I called him up.

"Look," I told him, "I'm closing the restaurant."

"Why are you telling me?" Danny asked.

To me it seemed obvious, but I spelled it out: "I like what you do. You like what I do. I think we should do something together."

Danny paused. "Tom, I'm sorry," he said, "but I'm never doing another restaurant again."

I hung up, disappointed but unfazed. Bob and I set out to find a new space. I was ready to scale up in size, which meant looking south. Downtown Manhattan in the early 1990s had many genteel pockets, but there were still neighborhoods with giant spaces to be had at a fair price. Although Rakel had faltered five years earlier, a number of restaurants were now thriving in SoHo and Tribeca, proving that uptown wallets were finally willing to brave the wilds of downtown for fine dining.

Once Mondrian closed, I lived like a normal person for the first time in fifteen years. I woke up with the sun in the morning and went to bed at a sensible hour at night. Kristen and I lived a fun inverse of an old-school relationship—she went to work at the bank, while I stayed home and cooked for us both. Where once I had thrived in chaos, I now relished the stability. Kristen was a few years older than me and wanted to start a family. I had just turned thirty, which seemed like as good a time as any; after all, by this age my parents had had all three of us. By early autumn of 1993, Kristen was pregnant, and I was over the moon.

And then, to my surprise, Danny called back. He'd had a change of heart. He told me he'd shared my idea with his good friend Robert Chadderdon, a wine importer with a finger on the pulse of New York dining, whose response was, "If Sandy Koufax called you and said he wanted to pitch for your team, you probably should say yes." I'd never been much of a baseball fan, but even I knew that was high praise indeed.

Danny suggested we get to know one another better before taking the leap into partnership. We decided to visit Italy together to see how we got along and whether our visions of a restaurant aligned. I had never been to Italy, but it was Danny's second home. His father owned a travel company back in St. Louis and so Danny had traveled regularly, visiting Italy often and even leading tours there as a teenager. He spoke the language and had a list of favorite restaurants for us to visit. We set off on a whirlwind itinerary through Piedmont, at the peak of truffle season. To my relief we found we were compatible travelers, taking off at times separately to explore, then meeting up again for dinner at night. I trawled through markets in old town squares, which were usually situated near an ancient church. I was thunderstruck at the beauty all around me, and at the incredible quality and simplicity of the food we encountered. Eating well in Italy wasn't reserved for special occasions. It was a daily given, its importance assumed. Ironically, as we ate together, Danny and I rarely talked about food. Instead, we shared our thoughts about life, our families, our vision for a future shared project. We envisioned a place where the food's technical excellence and daring would be matched to service that was equally elevated, but warm and free of pretension. Philosophically, we were in sync. When our week in Piedmont was over, we returned to New York excited to begin.

We continued my hunt for a space, visiting dozens of places, including the old Max's Kansas City on Park Avenue South and Andy Warhol's Factory at 860 Broadway. The most promising was an ancient showroom in the N. S. Meyer building on East 20th Street in the Flatiron District near Gramercy Park, which was occupied by a company that had been making medals for the United States military since the Civil War. The Flatiron District was still sketchy at night—just recently someone had been stabbed a few blocks south near Union Square—but it didn't take a genius to see that the neighborhood was swiftly changing. Magazines, book publishers, and modeling agencies were abandoning midtown for spacious offices in former warehouses and industrial spaces, and young professionals followed suit, trading the stolid Upper East and West Sides for bright modern lofts. The N. S. Meyer building's windows were boarded over with graffiti-covered plywood, but I could see that underneath they were magnificent. The space itself was perfect. It had twenty-foot ceilings and a combined ten thousand square feet over two floors: five thousand at street level for kitchen and dining, and another five thousand in the basement, which would be ideal for prep, pastry, offices, and wine storage. The owner, a guy named Bob Raeburn, wanted to keep part of the ground level for himself as a showroom, but Danny plied his famous charm over lunch at Union Square Cafe and talked him into giving us the full space. Danny even negotiated the rent down to $9,000 a month, a fraction of what we were paying at Mondrian, and locked us in for a twenty-year lease. We were in business.

With the space secured, we needed an architect, and Danny knew the ideal person: Peter Bentel, an innovative aesthete with a dignified mustache, who ran a family firm with his equally talented siblings. We'd settled on the name Gramercy Tavern. Taverns in America had historically served as gathering places for communities and weary travelers, and the word felt humble and appealingly fresh—New York City was already replete with cafés and bar and grills. Peter immediately grasped what we were going for—a design that merged rusticity and elegance in a way that felt timeless, as though it had been around for ages and would be for ages more. He proposed carving the cavernous raw space into three more intimate rooms, each with its own ceiling—coffered, beamed, and barrel vaulted. We hired an antiques dealer to scour flea markets and antiques stores up and down the East Coast, and they filled the space with objects and art that lent rich patina and interest to the decor. One of Danny's friends, the artist Robert Kushner, painted an eighty-foot jaw-dropper of a mural that colorfully featured local produce high along three walls of the bar. There was an open wood grill with its own menu in the bar area and a spacious private dining room able to accommodate forty guests at a time.

I threw myself into planning the menu and supervising the construction. This was the biggest project I had ever worked on, necessitating a small village of plumbers, electricians, millworkers, plasterers, and glaziers. I knew what I wanted, and what I didn't know, I learned from people whose craftmanship was as important to them as mine was to me. Everything took longer and cost more than expected, meaning we had to go back to our investors for additional funds. There were endless permits to be secured, applications to be filed, city inspections, and design revisions and reviews, a process that took over a year.

And then, a curveball: At thirty-two weeks, Kristen's blood pressure suddenly skyrocketed, and she was in grave danger unless the baby was delivered immediately. I scrubbed up and watched as Dante Sebastian Colicchio was born via C-section at NYU Hospital on April 21, 1994, weighing two pounds four ounces. As the neonatal team ferried him away, Kristen began to hemorrhage severely, and I stood by helplessly as doctors worked to staunch the bleeding. Once she was finally stabilized and wheeled to recovery, I went in search of our baby. NYU's NICU was full, so they had found an incubator for him a few blocks away at Bellevue Hospital. I tried to follow his gurney onto the ambulance but an orderly stopped me, per hospital rules. As the ambulance pulled out, I ran behind it on foot, weaving through traffic on First Avenue. It was one of those cold, rainy days of early spring, and I remember wiping the rain out of my eyes and running with everything I had to keep the ambulance in sight. Because I was wearing scrubs, no one at Bellevue stopped me as I followed the medics pushing him clear through the ER and up to the neonatal unit. I watched as a doctor bent over Dante, working to insert a catheter into a vein of his umbilical cord, and I'll never forget the look of relief on her face when at last she succeeded. I gazed at Dante in awe. Curled up, he was the size of my palm, covered head to foot in fine lanugo down, his skin stretched over tiny ribs and bones. The doctor looked up and noticed me for the first time. She scanned my wet scrubs, looking for an ID tag. "Who are you?" she asked. I pointed to Dante: "That's my son." I blinked back tears, using the word for the first time. She nodded and jerked her head toward the door, saying, "He's fine now. Go home and get some rest. You're going to need it."

Kristen was released from the hospital after four days. Dante remained in the NICU for seven weeks, fighting off infections and laboring to breathe with undeveloped lungs. Surfactant treatment had just been approved for preterm babies; the doctors told us had Dante been born a year or two earlier, he would have died of respiratory distress. They also told us there was a likelihood he would be blind, though a later brain scan showed that to not be true. The long weeks waiting for Dante to turn a corner awakened a frightening and unfamiliar feeling of vulnerability in me; my son was fragile, and therefore I was, too. Had my father felt this way when my brothers and I were born? Was this new fear going to be with me for life? When they finally let us take him home, Dante weighed a hefty (for him, for us) four pounds nine ounces. Friendly strangers would peek into his baby carriage and try to hide their alarm at his size, but Kristen and I were delighted. Four pounds nine ounces! We thought he looked great.

Kristen soon returned to work, and I dove into being Dante's dad. Mornings were our time together. Caring for him felt easy (it helped that the NICU nurses had trained him to sleep through the night). I'd strap Dante's tiny torso to mine and we'd wander the city together or I'd take him to Gymboree class. Fathers at Gymboree were still rare enough in 1994 that the moms would either offer to help me with diapering or eye me suspiciously, wondering why I wasn't at work. I would tuck Dante into a backpack baby carrier and take him with me for a day of fly-fishing in the Delaware River. He was wide-eyed, curious, and, despite his dramatic entrance, an easygoing little dude. In the afternoons, his babysitter Claire would take over and I'd head downtown to the tangle of wires and sawdust that was swiftly shaping up to become Gramercy Tavern.

Peter Kaminsky, a journalist, had been following us around for months, observing and taking notes for a story he'd pitched to the *New Yorker* offering an inside view of opening a New York City restaurant. At the last minute the staff at the *New Yorker* changed their mind, so Peter sold the story to *New York* magazine, whose angle was decidedly more sensationalistic. The magazine put us on the issue's cover, along with the question "Is This the Next 4 Star Restaurant?" The issue hit the stands on July 18, 1994, the same week we opened.

Danny and I were less than thrilled about this. For one thing, the article implied a certain cocky assumption on our part that we were "creating the Next Great New York Restaurant" (the magazine's words, not ours). Worse, it shone the brightest of lights on us from day one. Just as a hit play needs dress rehearsals to work out the kinks, most new restaurants—especially ones that have been built from scratch—benefit from a "soft opening," a few weeks under the radar of the press and public, to hit their stride. We were offering two separate full menus at Gramercy, an ambitious fine-dining menu and a second tavern menu up front in the bar room featuring dishes from

Me with Danny Meyer and Larry Goldenberg in 1994

the wood grill. Our pastry chef, the ridiculously talented Claudia Fleming, was new out of the gate, too, as this would be her first job as head pastry chef. Our front of house was a lively but unseasoned team of actors, writers, and artists, as far from Mondrian's Croatian mafia as you could get. If ever a restaurant would have benefited from a grace period, it was Gramercy Tavern. Thanks to Kaminsky's piece, any hope for that flew out the window.

The stakes weren't just high reputationally; this time I had skin in the game. Bob Scott had guaranteed a loan for me so that he and I could split 40 percent of the business, with the balance of shares owned by Danny and members of his family, who had insisted on a majority stake as a condition of their investment. I was now an owner. The good news: From the moment our doors opened, New Yorkers turned out in droves. Our reservationists were the hardest working in town, and my own phone rang around the clock; it felt like everyone I had ever met wanted a table. The bad news: It was sheer chaos. There was no ramp-up period. The dining room was filled to capacity nightly, the tavern teemed with walk-ins, and we had a waiting list for private parties from day one. On top of this, Danny's *Union Square Cafe Cookbook* had just come out, and he left on a book tour, leaving me and our general manager, Larry Goldenberg, to manage the hordes. Under me were two reliable and indefatigable sous-chefs I'd brought from Mondrian: Payson Dennis, a former army guy who'd once been stationed in the no-man's-land between North and South Korea, and Johnny Schaefer, a rock-steady pro who showed up early, got shit done, and never missed a single day of work in all the years I'd known him. Even with this pair, the volume made it impossible to cook at the level we had at Mondrian. We couldn't keep up with the numbers, and the pressure got to me. I was churlish and snappy, and I'd lose it when mistakes happened, yelling at staff in a way I'm not proud of today. I began to take shortcuts, dumbing down my food just enough to keep my head above water. I wasn't happy about it, but the goal—at least at the start—was simple survival.

In the frantic crush of bodies, we managed to miss Ruth Reichl, the *New York Times* food critic, who showed up incognito early in our run. When her review came out in October, she gave us two stars. Nothing to sneeze at, but a far cry from *New York*'s auspicious prediction. Reichl called the Tavern "a grand attempt to reinvent the American luxury restaurant." She praised the service, calling it "elegant without being formal and comfortable without being casual," but was critical of some of the cooking, finding some of the dishes bland or lacking cohesion, while other dishes earned high praise. Overall, Reichl had high hopes for us, concluding, "Eating at Gramercy Tavern is a bit like drinking a great wine when it is still in the barrel. You can almost taste the future, and it appears extremely promising. Gramercy Tavern has everything it takes to make a great restaurant. Except maturity."

Deep down I knew she was right, but going from three stars at Mondrian to two at Gramercy Tavern stung. The review led to some soul-searching. What kind of restaurant did I want Gramercy to be? What kind of chef—and human being—did I aspire to be? Had my lifelong itch for bigger! newer! more! caused me to lose sight of what I had been striving to develop all these years? Had my anxiety and ambition caused me to lose something integral about myself?

The *Times* review was a catalyst for change, but it wasn't the only one. The James Beard Awards were coming up in May, and I knew that, as the hot new kid on the block, Gramercy Tavern would be inundated with the best chefs from around the country, who typically dine out en masse the night before the awards ceremony. Did I want them thinking this was the best I could do?

But what were my options? I was getting crushed by the numbers. I felt helpless . . . until it dawned on me that I was still thinking like a cook, like an employee. As an owner, I had the agency to change course. I suggested to Danny that we take fewer reservations, thinning down the books from about forty reservations every half hour to twenty-two, a decrease of almost fifty percent. With a less frenetic pace, I argued, guests could relax into a more leisurely meal, perhaps order a second bottle of wine, and our check averages would rise. Fewer covers would also give us the breathing room to introduce tasting menus and specials, like a truffle prix fixe, that would catch the attention of New York's serious foodies and make up for the lower number of covers. Most importantly, fewer diners would allow me to cook up to my potential. I expected pushback from Danny and our partners. Surprisingly, there was none.

The change was instantaneous. Without the nightly crush, a boot was lifted from my neck, and I was able to cook like myself, take risks, even play a bit. I made my way back to the greenmarkets, often right at dawn when I'd have the run of the place, and then bring my haul a few blocks north to our kitchen, just as deliveries were arriving from our fishermen and meat purveyors. I would lay out everything on the prep counter and survey: fresh cod, scallops, John Dory, savoy cabbage, kale, a chaotic array of wild mushrooms. With the ingredients spread out in front of me, ideas would take rapid shape (I still do that today—seeing the physical food starts the ideas flowing). Soon my cooks would show up, grab coffee, and join me, and what a team they were. The top three jobs in our kitchen were held by hardworking women: Sarah Stegner and Sarah Wilson came on as additional sous-chefs, and the marvelously efficient Juliette Pope was our *saucier*. Claudia was a serious chef in her own right—her desserts were complex dishes that required real cooking and perfect technique. Our line cooks today read like a who's who of great American chefs—Matt Seeber, Marco Canora, James Tracey, Jonathan Benno, Christopher Albrecht, and Akhtar Nawab—but back then they were a bunch of young cooks hungry to learn, just as I had been at the Quilted Giraffe, Rakel, and Lou Mazuc. I'm awed by the talent of that kitchen: I could demonstrate a dish once and the team would immediately grasp it, their execution perfect. After those rocky first months we fell in sync and began moving like a single organism. To this day I'm grateful for each and every one of them and count them as friends. Every so often we give some young chef a heart attack by getting together at a new restaurant to share a meal and reminisce.

With support like that in the kitchen, I began to relax. My ADHD impulsivity helped me get creative with the wild variety of ingredients culled from the market, but now it was tempered by an adult

perspective and a deep reservoir of technique. My confidence grew to the point that I rarely tested a dish. No lengthy trials. What began its day in a crate from a fisherman or a sack from a farmer often found its way onto plates in a new dish that night. In short: I was cooking for myself again, and it was liberating.

The kitchen was running smoothly, but the front of house needed work. At Union Square Cafe, Danny had introduced an idea he called "enlightened hospitality," a concept that prioritized the emotional experience of the diner. The goal was to leave guests feeling great about their interaction with the restaurant. He and Steve Olson, Gramercy Tavern's service director, had hired a young group of charismatic and quirky individuals as captains and waiters. Most of them were proud of what we were attempting at Gramercy Tavern and took it seriously, but the same qualities that made these young people special often led to friction and a combustive energy. Our opening bedlam had depleted them, too, and things didn't improve when we explained we'd be doing fewer covers—meaning less income for them. Union Square Cafe was known for its long-serving waitstaff that more or less called the shots, but our system of service was more complex. It depended on cohesion and cooperation, which was often lacking. We moved to a tip pool model—all the tips were aggregated at the end of the night and distributed equitably based on position. This encouraged collaboration and a shared purpose—every guest on the floor was everyone's shared responsibility. I began staying late with the staff as they finished their side work and cashed out, getting to know them better so I could learn how to support them.

Slowly, the restaurant Danny and I had envisioned was taking shape. I became calmer and less prone to shouting. The food began to sing. Friendships developed and deepened among the staff. We had our first Christmas party at the dive bar next door and gathered for a picnic with all of our families for the Fourth of July. And then, as the fall of 1995 rounded into early 1996, we heard that Ruth Reichl had returned, incognito, for a second review, a rarity so soon after the first. The dining section was in Wednesday's paper, so I rushed up to the *New York Times* building in Midtown on Tuesday night after service to get my hands on an early edition. When I had it, I tore into the dining section and began to read:

> Mr. Colicchio's cooking has lost the tentative quality of the early days; he is now cooking with extraordinary confidence, creating dishes characterized by bold flavors and unusual harmonies. He seems to be trying to extract the essence of each ingredient, and he is fearless in following through.

The review went slowly through every dish on the menu, praising it all, including Claudia's incredible desserts. I rushed downtown, back to Gramercy, and spread the paper on the pass so everyone could read it for themselves. This time around, she gave us three stars. It was a powerful validation of what we had all been through together.

Looking back, it was an unbelievable moment. So many of my dreams were reaching fruition; I was now at the helm of a three-star restaurant that was attracting diners from around the world. I was a father to one of the cutest and brightest toddlers ever hatched (ask anyone). I had helped my mother buy her first home, a ranch in leafy Mountainside, New Jersey, which had always been her dream. I had every reason to be happy, but one.

The pressures of running Gramercy had taken a toll on my relationship. Kristen and I had grown apart, and I lacked the self-awareness and vocabulary to fix it. When Reichl wrote in her first review that the restaurant had everything it took to be great except maturity, she could have been writing about me. I conducted myself in relationships the same way I did everything else—by the seat of my pants. Without realizing it, I was playing by my father's rules: Put your head down and say little. By the winter of 1996 our silences had become a yawning chasm, and Kristen and I split up. As ever, the highs and the lows went hand in hand.

Summer
Recipes

Grilled Oysters with Calabrian Chile Butter

I love all oysters but prefer East Coast oysters for their brininess and, frankly, their proximity. It never makes sense to me that someone on the East Coast would eat West Coast oysters or vice versa. So this recipe calls for whatever oysters happen to be closest to you. At home in Mattituck, I use oysters from Peeko Oysters, Peter Stein's oyster farm in the Peconic Bay. In the summer, I grill these outside. In the winter, I like to make them in the fireplace indoors. I think the first time I made this I had some leftover Calabrian chile butter from another meal. The heat, the fat, and the brine went so well together that this has become something of a summer tradition.

Makes 12 oysters

1 dozen unshucked oysters	4 tablespoons Calabrian Chile Butter (recipe follows)

If you're using a charcoal grill, get it started. If you're using a gas grill, preheating can wait until closer to when you're ready to cook.

Vigorously scrub the oysters under cold running water to remove any dirt or debris.

One at a time, place an oyster on your work surface, cupped-side down. Dry the oyster and, using a folded-up kitchen towel, hold the oyster steady with your nondominant hand, with the hinge facing your dominant hand. Use the tip of an oyster knife to gently pry open the hinge, then twist and rotate the knife until the hinge pops open. Continue to pry, opening the oyster further. Wipe your blade clean as needed. Sweep the blade flat across the top of the oyster, gently slicing through the muscle that connects the oyster to the top shell. Remove and discard the top shell. Take care not to tip the oyster and lose the precious liquor inside the shell. Scrape the knife between the oyster and the bottom shell to sever the muscle attaching them, and set the shucked oyster, in the bottom shell, aside. Brush away any loose pieces of shell that may have fallen into the oyster.

Dab about 1 teaspoon of the butter mixture onto each oyster and carefully transfer the oysters, still in their bottom shells, to the grill. Cook, uncovered, just until the butter is melted and bubbling (mine took 2 to 4 minutes); the oysters will be warmed through and slightly cooked.

Use tongs to carefully transfer the oysters to a platter. Watch out for flare-ups as the butter drips out of the oysters. Serve immediately.

Calabrian Chile Butter

Use it on toast or in a pasta dish.

Makes about ½ cup

4 tablespoons unsalted butter, at room temperature
½ tablespoon chopped scallions
1½ teaspoons minced Lemon Confit (page 112)

1½ teaspoons crushed Calabrian chile pepper
2 tablespoons finely chopped shallot

In a medium bowl, combine the butter, scallions, lemon confit, Calabrian chile, and shallot and mash together until well incorporated. Store in the refrigerator for up to 4 weeks.

Chanterelles and Peaches with Summer Corn

A mushroom. A stone fruit. A vegetable (which is technically a fruit, but come on, corn should be a vegetable). On the surface, little unites chanterelles, peaches, and summer corn except that, at least in New York, you'll find them all appearing at markets around the same time of year, the late summer.

This recipe is a great example of what I would make at Gramercy Tavern, where we had close access to the Union Square Greenmarket, which was a big source of my inspiration. Once the ingredients were decided upon, we'd bring them back to the kitchen and the question would be: How do you approach them? Do you serve the corn raw, roasted, blanched, or maybe sautéed? Do you want the peaches cut and roasted or fresh, with herbs or no, perhaps pureed? And what are you serving with the salad?

For a late-summer salad, the dish rests on the sweetness of corn, the smokiness of bacon, and the umami of the chanterelles. It's perfect just the way it is. If, however, I were going to serve it with duck, I might want to reinforce the peach with acid to cut through the duck fat. I might puree the peaches to make a gastrique and use their skin for a tannin-rich demiglace for the sauce.

What starts off as a rudimentary combination of ingredients, a germ of an idea brought on by the fresh vegetables at the market, can be pushed and iterated upon until it feels complex or, as in this recipe, can be left in its simple yet addictive state.

Serves 2 to 4

2 teaspoons extra-virgin olive oil
2 small peaches, cut into wedges
2 tablespoons unsalted butter
1 teaspoon sugar
2 ounces slab bacon, cut into lardons

½ pound chanterelle mushrooms, cleaned and trimmed (torn into bite-size pieces if large)
Kosher salt
2 ears corn, kernels removed from the cob

2 scallions, green tops only,
  sliced, for garnish

2 fresh chives, sliced, plus more
  for garnish

Freshly ground black pepper

In a large skillet, heat the olive oil over medium-low heat. Add the peach wedges and sear on both sides, 2 to 3 minutes per side. Add 1 tablespoon of the butter and the sugar and continue to cook the peaches, agitating them occasionally so they don't stick, until caramelized, 2 to 3 minutes. Remove the peaches from the pan and set aside on a plate.

Clean the pan and return it to medium heat. Add the bacon and cook, stirring occasionally, until the fat has rendered and the bacon has started to crisp, about 5 minutes. Remove the bacon from the pan with a slotted spoon and set aside.

Add the chanterelles to the bacon fat in the pan. Season with salt. Cook the chanterelles, turning occasionally, until they get some color, 4 to 5 minutes. (You can deglaze with a tablespoon or two of water, if needed.)

Return the bacon to the pan and add the remaining 1 tablespoon butter. Add the corn kernels and cook until the corn is tender and everything has melded, 3 to 5 minutes.

In a bowl, combine the chanterelle mixture with the scallion greens and chives. Transfer to a platter, top with the peaches, and garnish with more chives. Season with salt and pepper and serve immediately.

Too Much Squash Fennel Salad

I make this salad to deal with the glut of zucchini and yellow squash that comes every summer. It really embodies what we try to do at Craft. I don't want to make the zucchini and squash taste like anything other than what they are. The technique here is meant to showcase the intrinsic flavor of the vegetable. In a recipe like this, the quality of your ingredients is really important. Here it's all about the zucchini. You'll want to find one that is about 4 inches long. Larger than that and zucchini can get too woody and stolid, with unpleasantly large seeds; smaller than that and there hasn't been enough time to develop flavor. The zucchini should feel dense to the touch without any bruising. The best way to tell whether a zucchini is fresh is to look at the stem end. If it's dry, the zucchini is old. Pick a better one.

Serves 8

3 large tomatoes (1 pound 10 ounces total)
1 shallot, finely diced
4 tablespoons extra-virgin olive oil
Kosher salt
2 zucchini (12 ounces total), thinly sliced on a mandoline
2 yellow squash (12 ounces total), thinly sliced on a mandoline

1 small red onion, sliced
Freshly ground black pepper
1 large or 2 small fennel bulbs, thinly sliced on a mandoline
Fresh basil leaves
2 tablespoons red wine vinegar

Using a box grater, grate 2 of the tomatoes into a bowl. Add the shallot and 2 tablespoons of the olive oil. Season with salt.

In a large bowl, combine the zucchini, yellow squash, and onion. Season generously with salt and pepper. Add the fennel and the remaining 2 tablespoons olive oil and mix together.

(recipe continues)

Slice the remaining tomato into wedges and gently fold into the zucchini and fennel mixture.

To serve, place the grated tomato at the bottom of a bowl or serving platter. Add the zucchini mixture. Top with fresh basil and the vinegar. Season with salt and pepper and serve immediately.

RFD Sour Cherry and Fennel Salsa

Once upon a time, I thought I'd write a gardening book. This recipe was inspired by two trips: one into my garden, where the lovage was flourishing; the other to the Mattituck farmers' market, where I was greeted by tables full of small scarlet sour cherries in their green containers. I immediately knew that the combination of lovage with its pronounced flavor and the tartness of cherries would make a tremendous salsa. The result was really f*$^ing delicious (RFD). This is a versatile recipe. You can use celery leaves if you can't find lovage and regular cherries if you can't find sour ones. (If using sweet cherries, add a little more vinegar to preserve the tartness.) I enjoy it as a summer salad, but it is maybe even better jarred and used a few days or even a month later as a condiment for grilled duck, chicken, or squab. It can also work with a heavier roasted fish like a grilled sardine.

Serves 4 to 6 as a side

4 cups (1¾ pounds) sour cherries, stemmed and pitted
½ cup chopped fresh cilantro
2 to 3 tablespoons chopped lovage or celery leaves
1 small fennel bulb, trimmed and very thinly sliced crosswise

4 scallions, sliced
½ jalapeño, thinly sliced into rings
½ cup extra-virgin olive oil
2 tablespoons sherry vinegar
Kosher salt and freshly ground black pepper

In a medium bowl, toss together the sour cherries, cilantro, lovage, fennel, scallions, and jalapeño rings. Fold in the olive oil and vinegar. Season with salt and generously with pepper. Toss everything together and serve.

The salad can sit for a couple of days in the fridge. It gets better with time. But if you want to make it ahead of time, leave out the cilantro until you are just about to serve.

Tenzin's Eggplant Salad

Though I don't cook with a lot of ginger in my restaurants, it's one of my favorite spices to use at home. This salad is a showcase for the bracing tang of ginger, the heat of the chiles, and, of course, the accommodating and suggestible eggplant. I first made the dish for our babysitter Tenzin who worked with us when the boys were young. She loved both eggplant and spicy foods; we loved her and her momos (dumplings). Now, even though Tenzin has a family of her own, I still think of her every time I make it.

Serves 4 to 6

½ cup extra-virgin olive oil

2 pounds small eggplants (mix of Japanese, fairytale, white), sliced on the diagonal into pieces ¾ to 1 inch thick

Kosher salt

2 long red peppers (preferably Anaheims), roughly chopped into large pieces

½ red onion, sliced

3 garlic cloves, sliced

1-inch knob fresh ginger, peeled and cut into matchsticks (2 tablespoons)

3 scallions, sliced

Freshly ground black pepper

Juice of 1 lime

2 tablespoons fish sauce

2 to 3 cups fresh herbs (aim for a mix of cilantro, Thai basil, basil, and parsley)

Line a large plate with paper towels. In a large heavy-bottomed pan, heat ¼ cup of the olive oil over medium-high heat. Working in batches and using more oil as needed, add the eggplant to the pan, season with salt, and stir-fry until browned on both sides, about 3 minutes per side. Transfer the eggplant to the paper towels.

Add the red peppers, onion, garlic, ginger, and scallions to the pan and season with salt and black pepper. Continue cooking over medium-high heat, agitating the pan every so often so the vegetables don't stick, until the peppers are charred in places and the onion is softened slightly, about 5 minutes.

(recipe continues)

Pour the pepper mixture into a bowl and add the eggplant. Add the lime juice and fish sauce and toss together. Top with half of the fresh herbs while the eggplant is still hot. Once the mixture has come to room temperature, finish with the remaining fresh herbs. Check the seasoning and serve.

Glazed White Turnips with Honey and Pink Peppercorns

To properly prepare these turnips, you have to understand how to use heat. Don't just blast it. (This is a common refrain in my restaurants, too. I frequently tell my cooks to lower the heat, even when their impulse is to crank it.) In this case, if you boil the hell out of the liquid, the liquid will reduce before the turnips are fully cooked. You want to be patient and understand what the liquid is doing as it reduces. It isn't simply making a glaze. It's also a cooking liquid. So be gentle, and you'll be rewarded.

Serves 4 as a side

4 bunches small white turnips (about 2 pounds)
8 tablespoons unsalted butter
1 shallot, sliced
½ cup honey

1½ teaspoons pink peppercorns, lightly crushed
2 tablespoons apple cider vinegar
Kosher salt

Trim off the turnip greens and set them aside. Cut any larger turnips in half.

In a sauté pan just wide enough to hold all the turnips in a single layer, melt 2 tablespoons of the butter over medium-low heat. When the butter has melted, add the shallot. Add the turnips and toss to coat.

Add the remaining 6 tablespoons butter, the honey, ½ cup water, and 1 teaspoon of the pink peppercorns. Bring to a boil, then reduce the heat to low and simmer, gently stirring every so often, until the turnips begin to soften, 15 to 20 minutes. Toward the end of the cooking time, the water should have mostly evaporated, leaving a honey and butter glaze. Right before the turnips are finished, add the vinegar. (If the turnips are tender before the liquid has reduced, transfer them to a plate with a slotted spoon and reduce the liquid until syrupy, then return the turnips to the pan and toss to coat.)

(recipe continues)

Set up a bowl with equal parts water and ice and have nearby. Bring a small pot of water to boil over high heat and season with salt. Add the turnip greens to the boiling water to blanch very briefly, 30 to 60 seconds. Quickly remove the leaves and drop them into the ice bath to stop the cooking. Drain well.

Add the blanched greens to the skillet and toss just to warm through. Season with salt and transfer to a serving bowl. Top with the remaining ½ teaspoon peppercorns.

Braised Zucchini with Black Olives

Too often zucchini recipes try to hide the taste of zucchini with a bunch of flavors. Why? Zucchini in season has a mild but wonderful flavor. This recipe dates back to my Gramercy Tavern days. I wanted a dish that actually tastes like zucchini. By quickly braising the vegetable in water (not stock), the flavor is intact, and set off by adding briny olives. When my zucchini are fresh from the garden, I'll add them right at the end. This dish goes well with a delicate protein like a piece of fish or with burrata. Stay away from roasted meats or anything that will overpower the flavors.

Serves 6 to 8 as a side

6 medium zucchini (about 2 pounds), seeded and cut into ½-inch cubes
Kosher salt
3 tablespoons extra-virgin olive oil
1 teaspoon finely grated lemon zest
2 teaspoons fresh lemon juice
3 sprigs fresh thyme
⅓ cup oil-cured black olives

To determine how much water you'll need, place the zucchini cubes in a pot big enough to hold them all and pour in water until it just barely covers the zucchini. Transfer the zucchini to a bowl using a large slotted spoon; what is left in the pot is the amount of water you'll need.

Bring the water to a simmer over medium-high heat. When the water is simmering, add the zucchini and generously season with salt. Cook, adjusting the heat as needed to maintain a simmer, until the zucchini is just tender, 7 to 10 minutes.

Add the olive oil, lemon zest, lemon juice, and thyme and gently stir. Check the seasoning. Remove from the heat, add the olives, and toss together.

To serve, if serving as a side dish, drain the zucchini to remove excess water. If using atop a piece of fish, for example, it's okay to leave the zucchini a little brothy.

It's Corn; It's Got the Juice

You don't have to do much to corn to make it delicious. Sweet Jersey corn tastes best eaten raw off the cob just after picking it on a hot day. But when you cook it in butter, the corn . . . well, of course corn and butter go together. No need to explain. The other key ingredient in this is chili crisp, a readily available condiment, which I'd put on everything if I could. (And at home, I do.) Here the crunch and the jalapeño round out the sweetness of the corn and honey.

Serves 4 to 6 as a side

4 tablespoons unsalted butter
6 ears corn, shucked
¼ cup honey
2 to 3 tablespoons chili crisp, to taste
Kosher salt

½ jalapeño, thinly sliced into rings
2 scallions, sliced
1 lime, quartered
Chopped fresh cilantro, for serving

In a large pan that will fit all the corn (you can use a roasting pan or cook the corn in batches if it doesn't all fit), warm the butter over medium-low heat. Once the butter has melted, place the corn in the pan and cook until the kernels just start to get some color on all sides, turning every so often, 5 to 8 minutes.

Add the honey and chili crisp to the pan and season with salt. Baste over the corn until the honey starts to caramelize, 1 to 2 minutes. Add the jalapeño and scallions. Continue to turn the corn until the sauce has reduced and the corn is tender, 2 to 3 minutes.

Serve hot with a squeeze of lime and a sprinkling of fresh cilantro.

Chickpea Seafood Salad

There's not a coastal town in Northern Italy that doesn't have some version of a chickpea seafood salad. Seafood is abundant and chickpeas grow plentifully, and what grows together goes together. In this salad, the general mechanic is that the starch of the chickpeas works well to soak up and complement the seafood. At the restaurant, we use octopus and leftover lobster knuckles. At home, I make this salad with whatever seafood I have around, usually a bunch of shrimp. If you're inclined, you can add some potatoes, too—fingerlings work well—cooled down and tossed with the rest of the ingredients.

Serves 4 to 6 as a side

Two 16-ounce cans chickpeas, drained and rinsed
½ cup diced celery
½ cup sliced red onion
1 small tomato, seeded and sliced
1 tablespoon minced Lemon Confit (page 112)
½ tablespoon minced Garlic Confit (page 113)
1 teaspoon crushed Calabrian chile pepper
½ fresh Fresno chile, sliced

Kosher salt and freshly ground black pepper
2 tablespoons extra-virgin olive oil, plus more for drizzling
10 to 12 large shrimp, peeled and deveined, tails left on
1 cup loosely packed fresh parsley leaves, roughly chopped
1 teaspoon dried oregano
Grated zest and juice of 1 lemon

In a large bowl, combine the chickpeas, celery, onion, tomato, lemon confit, garlic confit, Calabrian chile, and Fresno chile. Season with salt and black pepper and mix together. Set aside while you prepare the shrimp.

In a large sauté pan, heat the olive oil over medium heat until shimmering. Season the shrimp with salt and black pepper. Add the shrimp to the pan and cook until opaque, 2 to 3 minutes. Turn the shrimp and let them cook until opaque on the second side, another 2 to 3 minutes.

Add the shrimp to the chickpea salad. Mix in the parsley, oregano, lemon zest, lemon juice, and a drizzle of olive oil. Season with salt and pepper to taste and serve.

Storage: The salad is best served at room temperature the day it's made. If you're keeping it for another day, don't add the herbs until right before serving. The acid in the dressing will turn the leaves brown.

My First Recipe: Mussels with Tomatoes, Tarragon, and Red Onion

Mussels might seem like a weird thing for a kid to cook, but when I read the recipe for Pierre Franey's Mussels Vinaigrette in *The New New York Times Cookbook*, I decided to create my own take on it. The liquid in which you cook the mussels becomes the sauce. Over the years, I've made some modifications like adding the tomatoes and Calabrian chile. But the simplicity and deliciousness of the preparation that drew me to the dish when I was a teenager still keep me coming back to it forty-plus years on. Serve with crusty toasted bread.

Serves 4

2 large tomatoes (2 pounds 5 ounces), cored and cut into a medium dice
¾ cup extra-virgin olive oil
2 tablespoons red wine vinegar
1 shallot, finely diced
Grated zest of 1 lemon
Kosher salt and freshly ground black pepper
1 tablespoon crushed Calabrian chile pepper (optional)

2 pounds mussels
½ red onion, sliced
3 garlic cloves, sliced
1 cup white wine
1 bunch scallions, green tops only, sliced
½ cup chopped fresh parsley
3 to 4 sprigs fresh tarragon, chopped (3 packed tablespoons)

In a bowl, mix the tomatoes with ½ cup of the olive oil and the vinegar, shallot, and lemon zest. Season with salt and black pepper. Add the Calabrian chile if you want the dish to have a little heat. Let the mixture sit while you cook the mussels.

Place the mussels in a bowl of cold water and remove any fibrous beards. Wash in cold water, agitating with your hand to remove any remaining sand and debris. Rinse well. Any mussels that are open and do not close when you tap on them should be thrown away.

In a large pot, warm the remaining ¼ cup olive oil over medium heat. When the oil is hot, add the onion and let it sweat until translucent, 5 to 7 minutes.

Add the garlic and cook for 3 to 5 minutes. Pour in the white wine, season with salt, and add the mussels. Cover the pot with a tight-fitting lid and steam the mussels until they open, about 8 minutes. Discard any mussels that don't open.

Remove the mussels from the heat and transfer to a large bowl with a slotted spoon. Allow the mussels to cool completely (they can be placed in the refrigerator to speed the process).

Pour the tomato mixture into the bowl with the mussels. Add the scallion greens, parsley, and tarragon. Season with salt and black pepper. Mix together and serve.

Squid with Almost but Not Quite Burst Cherry Tomatoes

This dish is ideal in late summer when you have lots of tomatoes. After quickly pan-roasting these cherry tomatoes, they plump up into little flavor grenades. You want the tomatoes to be on the point of bursting but not ready to fully explode. They should release their delicious warm and sweet juice when you bite into them, not into the dish itself. The key to that is, as always, being judicious with the heat. You want to poach the tomatoes in just barely simmering liquid.

Serves 4

⅓ cup extra-virgin olive oil, plus more for drizzling

2½ pounds mixed cherry tomatoes

2 large garlic cloves, minced

Kosher salt and freshly ground black pepper

1½ pounds small squid, cleaned, bodies cut into ⅓-inch rings and tentacles halved

1½ tablespoons white wine vinegar

1 cup lightly packed small fresh basil leaves

Flaky salt

Grilled bread, for serving

In a large sauté pan, heat the olive oil over medium heat until shimmering. Add the tomatoes, garlic, and a pinch of salt and pepper. Cook, stirring, until the tomatoes just start to blister, 3 to 4 minutes.

Season the squid with salt and pepper. Stir the squid into the tomatoes and reduce the heat to low. Cook, stirring occasionally, until the squid turns opaque and the tomatoes soften slightly, about 5 minutes. The tomatoes should be lightly cooked but mostly maintain their shape; they shouldn't turn to sauce. Stir in the vinegar and basil and season with salt and pepper.

Divide the tomato and squid among bowls and drizzle with olive oil, flaky salt, and more fresh pepper. Serve immediately, with grilled bread alongside.

Star-Spangled Squid Rice

Some travelers collect snow globes and magnets from their trips; I bring back recipes. This squid rice comes from a long-ago trip that Dante, Lori, and I took to Spain. We dropped Dante off at a teen travel program in Barcelona and then Lori and I continued to Cáceres in Extremadura for a few days of vacation. Every restaurant there served some version of black rice with squid or seafood and plenty of herbs. The paella-type dish seemingly contained the flavors of the Mediterranean in one effortless meal. Back home I brought out a paella pan and re-created the squid rice over the grill for our posse of summer friends in Mattituck. (You can make it as easily in a skillet on the stovetop.) The dish quickly became a party favorite that kicks off our summer.

Serves 4

4 tablespoons Blond Sofrito
  (page 109)
8 ounces squid, cleaned, bodies
  sliced into rings
Kosher salt
2 garlic cloves, chopped
1 scallion, sliced
1½ cups bomba rice
3 cups chicken stock, at room
  temperature

1½ tablespoons squid or
  cuttlefish ink (see Notes)
Freshly ground black pepper
Aioli (optional; page 253), for
  serving
Chopped fresh cilantro, for
  garnish

In a large pan, warm the sofrito over medium heat for about 5 minutes. Add the squid to the sofrito, season with salt, and mix together. Add the garlic and scallion to the pan and cook until fragrant, about 1 minute. Pour the rice into the pan and stir together with the squid.

Meanwhile, in a large measuring cup or bowl, combine the chicken stock and squid ink and mix together. Add the stock mixture to the pan with the rice. Mix everything together and season with salt and pepper. Bring to a boil, then reduce the heat to a simmer and cook, uncovered, until the rice is tender and has absorbed almost all the stock, 20 to 25 minutes (see Notes).

Remove from the heat, cover, and let sit 10 minutes. Serve with aioli if desired and garnish with cilantro.

Storage: Leftover squid rice can be kept covered in the refrigerator for 2 to 3 days.

Notes:

- Buy squid ink, if you can find it, but most commercially available squid ink is actually the milder ink from cuttlefish, another cephalopod. It tastes mostly the same.

- If the rice isn't cooked through at this point, just add some more stock and continue to cook.

Aioli

Aioli can sometimes be overpoweringly garlicky, but by using confit here, you get the sweetness of garlic without the sharpness. The lemon confit and the lemon juice add a burst of bright acid. Because this is so easy to make, I always have some on hand. I think of it as an instant sandwich flavor enhancer.

Makes 1 cup

1 egg yolk
2 tablespoons finely chopped
 Lemon Confit (page 112)
2 tablespoons finely chopped
 Garlic Confit (page 113)

Juice of ½ lemon
1 cup extra-virgin olive oil
Kosher salt

In a medium bowl, whisk together the egg yolk, lemon confit, garlic confit, and lemon juice. Whisking constantly, slowly pour in the oil. The mixture will begin to thicken. If the aioli becomes too thick, thin with a bit of water and continue mixing. After the oil has been fully incorporated, taste for seasoning and add salt accordingly.

Storage: The aioli will keep in an airtight container in the refrigerator for up to 1 week.

Lazy Summer Pasta

As any vegetable gardener knows, during the late summer you're going to have more eggplant, zucchini, and tomatoes than you can possibly use. I give some to my neighbors in Mattituck. I make jars and jars of tomato sauce. And still . . . I'm left with mounds of highly perishable produce. Happily, this recipe, which is essentially a ratatouille plus pasta, eats up a lot of veggies and makes a super-simple and delicious dinner only steps removed from the garden. Technically, it's important here to add the vegetables in batches. The key to successfully sautéing is maintaining a steady pan temperature. If you were to add all the vegetables at once, the temperature would drop and you'd be sweating, not sautéing. You want a little color, which imbues the veggies with sweetness, but not so much that you can taste the char.

Serves 4 to 6

Kosher salt
¾ to 1 cup extra-virgin olive oil
1 red onion, halved and thinly
  sliced
1 red bell pepper, thinly sliced
1 fennel bulb, halved and thinly
  sliced
1 zucchini, cut into ¼-inch dice
1 medium/large eggplant,
  partially peeled, cut into
  ¼-inch dice

2 garlic cloves, thinly sliced
1 dry pint cherry tomatoes,
  halved
1 pound fusilli pasta
¾ cup freshly grated pecorino
  cheese
½ cup chopped fresh basil
½ cup chopped fresh parsley
Freshly ground black pepper

Bring a large pot of salted water to a boil for the pasta. Meanwhile, prepare the vegetables.

In a large pot, heat 3 tablespoons of the olive oil over medium-low heat. Add the onion and season with a bit of salt. Cook, stirring occasionally, until the onion is just slightly translucent, about 5 minutes. Add the bell pepper and fennel and stir gently. After

5 minutes, add the zucchini and stir gently. Let cook for another 5 minutes and then, working in batches, add the eggplant. Add more olive oil as needed to prevent burning as you add the eggplant. The eggplant will start to break up as you mix everything together. Keep seasoning with salt as you go.

Add the garlic to the pan last. Mix everything together and cook until the vegetables are soft and combined but still retain some shape. At this point, the vegetables should have been cooking for a total of 15 to 20 minutes. Finally, add the tomatoes, mix until they burst, about 5 minutes, then remove from the heat.

Add the fusilli to the boiling water and cook to al dente according to the package directions.

Reserving 1 cup of the pasta water, drain the pasta and add to the vegetables. Over low heat, slowly combine all together. Add ½ cup of the grated pecorino and the basil and parsley. Add just enough pasta water, a little at a time, to bring the pasta and vegetables together. Season with salt and black pepper to taste and top with the remaining pecorino. Serve right away.

Eat Your Greens Pasta

This leafy greens pasta is made with kale, spigarello, *and* Swiss chard. But it could be a leafy greens pasta with kale or spigarello or Swiss chard . . . or whatever other leafy greens you can get. Or you might not include the pasta at all. Take away the pasta and this could be, on its own, a side dish for a roast meat or a fish. Add some beans to this and you get pasta fagioli. Add some broth to the beans and you have a hearty soup. Learn to move your ingredients around and vary the proportions. The possibilities are endless. This recipe is a call to improvise with the ingredients you have and to recognize how versatile they are.

Serves 4

Kosher salt
7 to 8 tablespoons extra-virgin
  olive oil
10 ounces guanciale, chopped
1 small red onion, halved and
  sliced
1 small fennel bulb, halved,
  cored, and chopped
Freshly ground black pepper
2 garlic cloves, minced
1 bunch lacinato kale, tough
  stems removed and leaves
  roughly chopped

1 bunch spigarello, tough stems
  removed and leaves roughly
  chopped
1 bunch green Swiss chard,
  tough stems removed and
  leaves roughly chopped
1 pound paccheri pasta or any
  pasta shape you want
½ cup freshly grated pecorino
  cheese

Bring a large pot of salted water to a boil over high heat. While the water is boiling, prepare the vegetables.

In a large pot, warm 4 tablespoons of the olive oil over medium heat. Add the guanciale, onion, and fennel. Mix together and season with salt and pepper. Cook, stirring occasionally, until the fennel and onion are soft and translucent, roughly 4 to 5 minutes. Add the garlic and cook until fragrant, about 30 seconds.

Start adding the kale, spigarello, and Swiss chard in batches. The greens will wilt down as they cook, allowing you to add more to the pan. Mix the greens together with the onion as you go. Cook the greens until fully wilted, 4 to 5 minutes. Check the seasoning, adding salt if necessary.

Add the pasta to the boiling water and cook until al dente according to the package directions. Reserving 1 cup of the pasta water, drain the pasta.

Add the cooked pasta to the pot with the greens. Combine and toss with ⅓ cup of the reserved pasta water, the remaining 3 to 4 tablespoons olive oil, and grated pecorino until the sauce becomes creamy. Season generously with pepper and salt to taste. Serve.

Storage: This pasta will keep in the fridge for 1 or 2 days.

Quick Summer Pasta with Cherry Tomatoes and Red Onions

This quick summer pasta relies on the sweetness of the tomatoes and onions playing off the heat from the Calabrian chile and the herby notes of the basil and parsley. As always, the exact amounts are up to you. (Are you a basil fanatic? Fine. Just keep in mind you'll need to structure your ratios so the basil isn't overpowering.) Though amounts don't matter much, what *is* important is technique. Here the main technique is cooking pasta. Don't overcook the pasta. You can have the most exquisitely balanced flavors, but if you have overcooked pasta flopping around like a limp noodle, the flavors hardly matter.

Serves 4 to 6

Kosher salt
¼ cup extra-virgin olive oil
1 red onion, sliced
2 dry pints cherry tomatoes
1 tablespoon crushed Calabrian chile pepper

1 cup roughly chopped fresh parsley
3 garlic cloves, sliced
1 pound bucatini pasta
1 cup chopped fresh basil
Freshly ground black pepper

Bring a large pot of salted water to a boil over high heat for the pasta.

Meanwhile, in a large sauté pan, heat the olive oil over medium heat. Add the onion and season with salt. Cook, stirring occasionally, until translucent, 5 to 7 minutes. Add the cherry tomatoes and stir together. Add the Calabrian chile. Add ½ cup of the parsley and the garlic and mix. Let everything stew together until the tomatoes begin to release their juices, 5 to 6 minutes. (You can cover the pan briefly if needed to urge the tomatoes along.)

(recipe continues)

While the tomatoes are stewing, add the bucatini to the boiling water and cook, stirring occasionally, until al dente according to the package directions.

Reserving 1 cup of the pasta water, drain the pasta, then add the cooked pasta to the pan with the tomatoes. Add the remaining ½ cup fresh parsley and the basil and stir together. Season generously with salt and black pepper. Add a few tablespoons of reserved pasta water if needed to achieve a silky sauce. Taste for seasoning and serve.

Eggplant Parm That's Not a Pain in the Ass and Gluten-Free for Those Who Are

Breading eggplant is a pain in the ass. One summer, I just decided I had had enough. I'm not gonna do it anymore. No one complained. In fact, when you have really good eggplant, simply frying it (in really good olive oil) lets the eggplant shine through. This dish is meant to be easy to make and to feed a lot of people. (It keeps well for a week.) If you don't feel like making tomato sauce, don't. Using 5 to 6 cups of store-bought stuff is fine. Also, you'll notice I don't mess with leaching the eggplant with salt, a common technique. I don't find it necessary. Finally, after much experimentation, I realized that though it seems like a good idea to use fresh mozzarella—who doesn't like fresh mozzarella?—low-moisture, i.e., packaged mozzarella, works best or else the sauce gets too watery.

Serves 8 to 10

Three 28-ounce cans whole tomatoes, undrained

2 to 3 cups plus 2 tablespoons extra-virgin olive oil

1 garlic clove, sliced

½ medium yellow onion, finely diced

Kosher salt

3 sprigs fresh thyme

Freshly ground black pepper

3½ pounds eggplants (3 to 4 medium), partially peeled and sliced into rounds ¼ inch thick

1 pound low-moisture mozzarella cheese, thinly sliced

¾ cup grated Parmesan or pecorino cheese

Using a food mill or a food processor, process the whole tomatoes, with their juices, until lightly chopped. Add ½ cup water to one of the tomato cans and swirl out any remaining juices, then use the same water for the remaining cans. Add this water to the chopped tomatoes.

(recipe continues)

263

In a pot large enough to hold the tomatoes, heat 2 tablespoons of the olive oil over medium heat until warm. Add the garlic and cook for 1 minute. Add the diced onion, season with salt, and cook, stirring, until fragrant, 3 to 4 minutes.

Pour all of the tomatoes into the pot. Add the thyme. Season with salt and pepper. Let the sauce simmer over low heat until it is thickened and the flavors meld, about 1 hour, while you prepare the eggplant.

Line a sheet pan with paper towels and keep near the stove. In a large sauté pan, heat ½ cup of the olive oil over medium heat until shimmering. Working in batches, add a few slices of eggplant to the oil and season with salt. Fry, turning occasionally, until lightly browned on both sides, 6 to 8 minutes total. Transfer to the paper towels and season lightly with salt. The eggplant will soak up a lot of oil while it cooks. Continue to cook the eggplant, adding about ¼ cup more oil to the pan per batch. Continue until all the eggplant slices have been browned.

Preheat the oven to 350°F.

In a 9 × 13-inch baking dish, spoon a ladle (2 cups) of tomato sauce into the pan and spread it out so the bottom of the pan is covered. Place a layer of eggplant slices in the pan, laying them in like shingles. Follow with a layer of mozzarella slices. Add a sprinkling of grated cheese. Repeat the layers in this fashion until all the ingredients are used (set a little Parmesan aside). The top layer should end with tomato sauce (see Note).

Bake the eggplant Parmesan, uncovered, until bubbling and hot, about 1 hour. Toward the end of the cooking time, sprinkle with the reserved Parmesan and let cook a few more minutes.

Allow the eggplant to sit for about 1 hour before serving.

Note: If you have extra sauce, which you will, freeze separately and use later. The eggplant keeps covered in the fridge for up to 5 days and frozen for up to 3 months.

———

9

Nowhere to Hide

CRAFT BEGAN WITH a phone call.

"Tom," said Bob Bracco, a neighbor who was the head of a condo board for a building on East 19th Street, "do you have a second to come up and talk to me about trash?"

"Are you kidding?" I said. "I love talking trash."

We were eight years into Gramercy Tavern at the time. After that rough first year, we had found our footing and become a mainstay of New York dining, routinely taking the #1 or #2 spot in Zagat for New Yorkers' most popular restaurant (alternating with Union Square Cafe). In 2000 the James Beard Foundation named me the best chef in New York and gave Claudia the award for outstanding pastry chef (we also received awards for best service, a testament to our staff's incredible professionalism and kindness). Word had spread beyond New York City, and Gramercy Tavern played host to increasing numbers of diners from all over the world. Come summer, which is typically a slow season for New York restaurants, we were jammed with visitors, folks who had read about us and made Gramercy a special destination.

Somewhere in there I'd been named one of *Bon Appétit*'s best chefs, and the restaurant was profitable. Life was good, I was busy, and Bob seemed like a nice guy—plus, the building was just one block south.

Bob was in the process of turning a former department store at 47 East 19th Street into a restaurant. Then, as now, the regulatory hassle was substantial. He wanted to talk through basics like trash collection, HVAC, and permitting. I was happy to answer as best I could, checking out the space as we talked. I could see that, at 5,400 square feet, it would make one hell of a restaurant. "You know, Bob," I said, "if you're looking for a tenant, I'd be interested."

"Sorry, Tom," Bob answered. "It's spoken for." Fine, I thought. But after a couple of months with no apparent movement behind the plate glass windows, I gave Bob a call. "The guy that was supposed to take it fell through," he said. "But now Geoffrey Zakarian's coming in." Geoffrey, who had won three stars from the *New York Times* at Patroon, was looking for a space for his own restaurant. I guess he'd found it.

I didn't lose sleep over it. I was already losing sleep, but that was because I had fallen in love with a captain at Gramercy, an aspiring filmmaker who was finishing up her master's degree at NYU. Lori and I routinely stayed up until dawn talking about everything under the sun—politics, family, philosophy, you name it. She was the full package—a former model who read the *New York Times* cover to cover daily. She was empathetic and hilarious and just as opinionated and fiery as I was—our fights were as epic as our fun—and I knew right away that this was the relationship I had been waiting for my whole life. Best of all, she adored Dante, couldn't get enough of him, and the feeling was mutual.

Me with Dante, age 4

Being head over heels is distracting, which was maybe why I didn't grasp the extent of the friction growing between me and Danny Meyer. Part of it stemmed from a new set of partners Danny had brought in, one of whom I felt was looking to cut corners in ways that went against Gramercy's values. I was also eager to capitalize on Gramercy Tavern's success by opening a second location, while Danny resisted. Over the years these issues had sporadically surfaced, but recently they had come to a head.

Danny hosted a company retreat in Bucks County, Pennsylvania, an idyllic area of rolling hills and forests a few hours outside New York City. The leadership teams of Gramercy and Union Square Cafe were there, which included Michael Romano, the chef at Union Square Cafe, and Paul Bolles-Beaven, the general manager, both of whom I knew quite well, but also the two new partners Danny was onboarding. Richard Coraine, who had worked with Wolfgang Puck and had been a partner in a restaurant in San Francisco, was the new director of operations. David Swinghamer, who had previously worked for the Chicago restaurant group Lettuce Entertain You, was the new CFO. Together we'd all begun collaborating on two new restaurants in the MetLife building: Eleven Madison Park, a new American restaurant concept, and Tabla, a fine-dining Indian restaurant with Floyd Cardoz, the gifted Mumbai-born chef who had worked under Gray Kunz at Lespinasse. I had brought my good friend Kerry Heffernan in as chef for Eleven Madison Park, and I worked with Floyd on Tabla's kitchen design.

A woman I didn't recognize was at the meeting. Danny kicked things off with an announcement: He was starting a new company, which he planned to call Union Square Hospitality Group. Fine, I thought, that makes sense. I would have appreciated a heads-up, but okay. With Eleven Madison and Tabla on the way, now was as good a time as any to turn the collection of restaurants into a more formal group.

Then Danny went on to explain the ownership. He would own 51 percent of the company and divvy up the remaining 49 percent among the rest of us, with the lion's share going to Richard and David, the two new partners. Paul, Michael, and I would split the rest. My ownership, after I had built Gramercy into a critical and financial juggernaut that would help power this new venture, was to be 2 percent. I sat there, processing this, even as Danny continued: To cover Coraine and Swinghamer's salaries and fund operations, Gramercy Tavern and

Union Square Cafe would pay a management fee to this new company. Record scratch. What? Gramercy Tavern was running like a Swiss watch. We were winning awards, breaking records, making news, and making money. Why should we start paying for new "management"? Danny delivered the news in his typical sunny Midwestern way, but the Jersey street kid in me wasn't having it. I stood up, furious: "What is this bullshit? Absolutely not." I looked around to see who else found this laughable. To my amazement, no one else said a word. It seemed they were all familiar with the plan.

The woman, hitherto silent, piped up disapprovingly. "Danny," she said, identifying herself as a professional mediator, "you were meant to talk to Tom about this before the meeting. Clearly you didn't." No, he hadn't.

I felt blindsided, my mind roiling with questions. What about the other partners who had been instrumental in funding Gramercy's opening, like Bob Scott? Were they going to be left out in the cold while two new and unproven suits benefited from the risk these partners had undertaken on our behalf? The stars and critical acclaim Gramercy Tavern had won would burnish Union Square Hospitality Group from day one, immediately giving it credibility with funders and future diners alike. Wouldn't a more equitable solution be to get outside valuations on Gramercy Tavern and Union Square Cafe and then determine pro rata shares from there? Bob and I were Danny's largest partners, owning 40 percent of Gramercy Tavern between us—how did that translate to 2 percent of a new company growing from the seeds of what we'd planted?

What stung the most was that, up until that moment, where Danny was concerned, I had always thought of Gramercy Tavern as "our thing"—our shared baby, if you will, and our partnership as a manifestation of a real friendship and shared vision for the future. I had been wrong. Though we'd succeeded beyond our wildest hopes, the upside that "our thing" had now made possible—an expanding restaurant group primed for growth—was not an "us" thing. It was a Danny thing.

After the retreat, Danny and I let things cool off a bit, and I mulled it over. David Swinghamer asked me and the rest of the group to sign on to a joint and several loan agreement for $3 million that USHG was borrowing to open Eleven Madison Park and Tabla. This meant that each partner of USHG—no matter how minor a shareholder—could be held legally responsible for the entire debt if anything went wrong. That cinched the thing for me. If anything went south, I could be on the hook for their debt load as a 2 percent owner. I called Danny, and we came to an agreement. I told him I wouldn't be moving ahead with USHG, though I was happy to help out when needed. We would continue as partners at Gramercy, and I'd carry on with my own future projects. Everyone else from the retreat signed the USHG deal. Things were amiable enough on the surface. But a germ of mistrust had taken root. Later that year, Bob Raeburn offered us a lease for the second floor above Gramercy Tavern's dining room, which he'd been using as a storeroom. We had been turning away private event business for years, and the additional five thousand square feet on offer would have increased revenues by about $6 million a year. To me, it was a no-brainer. David Swinghamer had a different idea, though, explaining that the restaurant group was too busy at the time opening Eleven Madison Park and Tabla to take on such a big project. I suggested we slow-walk negotiations with the landlord; after all, the space had no value to anyone but us. Again, the answer was no. I suggested we carry the lease—it was a steal at $9,000 a month—until we were ready to build it out. Swinghamer and Danny were flat-out uninterested, even though it was clearly in Gramercy's best interest. Could it be that they were fending off competition for Eleven Madison Park, which had its own private event space in the works? Or that Swinghamer, who was not a partner in Gramercy Tavern, saw no upside for himself in its growth?

So when Bob Bracco called again to say Zakarian had pulled out, I told him I wanted the space on 19th Street. I would have taken it even without the dust-up with Danny. For some time, the old itch to take on something new had been wending its way into my thoughts. You could draw a straight line from Quilted Giraffe through Rakel to Mondrian to the food I was doing at Gramercy Tavern, but now I felt myself paring things down, trying to see what I could remove from the plate, while still retaining the essence of the dish. I was evolving—starting with the way I myself ate. I was finding myself more impressed by a perfectly cooked egg than an elaborate tower of food.

Each spring the James Beard Awards, the so-called Oscars of the culinary world, would bring the country's best chefs to New York City. I decided to host an informal dinner after the ceremony to fuel us before the night's long round of parties. Johnny Schaefer was now my chef de cuisine, and he and I planned the menu. "Just serve it family-style," I told John. "We don't need to bother with settings. We're just going to walk in, help ourselves, and leave."

Walking into the private room that night after the ceremony, I saw that my team had executed perfectly: Waiting for us was a simple platter of baby lamb—roasted loin, rack and leg, braised tongue—dressed in nothing but a light jus with olive oil and thyme. Alongside were a bowl of glistening butter-braised morels, a platter of roasted ramps, and a bowl of bright spring peas at the height of their sweetness. Our guests showed up, including Thomas Keller, Alfred Portale, Grant Achatz, and Frank Crispo, among others, and began to tuck in. They were eating with enthusiasm, savoring the freedom of helping themselves to whatever they wished, the relaxation of eating simply, without an elaborate presentation standing in the way. I remember thinking, "This is it. This is what I want to do next."

As the idea for Craft took shape, I remained deeply committed to Gramercy. Interestingly, the two restaurants functioned as creative counterpoints to one another. My cooking at Gramercy helped me hone in on exactly what I wanted Craft to be. Every element on the plate at Gramercy, no matter how small relative to the larger dish, was prepared to the highest standard and then juxtaposed with other elements on the plate to create interest. At Craft we were laser-focused on the execution—the cooking *itself*—as the wow factor. Flavor was everything. The only thing. After working on the menu for Craft, I'd head to the pass at Gramercy, exuberant all over again about the complexity and finesse of Gramercy's menu. The ADHD brain flourishes when it fires on all cylinders, and I remember this as a time of happy inventiveness as I seamlessly moved between concepts, each feeding the other.

With the lease on 19th Street signed, architect Peter Bentel and I dove deep into transforming the space. We wanted the look and feel of Craft to reflect the culinary philosophy within its walls. Just as the ingredients on Craft's menu were to be presented simply and without artifice, so would the building materials and construction. We wanted a design that felt elemental, one that revealed rather than obfuscated.

Inspired by artist Richard Serra, we built a sloped curving wall clad in leather and Brazilian black walnut along one side of the long and narrow dining room that connected the front and back of the space. We built a double-height wine vault from humble components like bronze, steel, and wood and made it visible to diners, who from their seats could watch their server climb the steps and collect their choice. We stripped the plaster off columns to reveal the beautiful terra-cotta underneath, which lent a wash of warmth throughout the

space without the need for paint, and let the walls and floors float against one another without the frippery of moldings. We left as many surfaces unvarnished as we could—stripped of their disguises, the building materials carried a rustic beauty all their own, just as a perfect mushroom or radish or sea scallop does before sauces and garnish. I had always loved the look of Edison bulbs—in which the filaments are both utility and design—and we placed dozens into our chandeliers. Now they're commonplace, but they were so unique and remarked upon at the

time that we turned one into Craft's logo. Bob Scott had a grove of cherry trees on his farm in Vermont, and we hired an artisan to craft some of them into tables so beautiful we canceled our tablecloth order.

When I was at Gramercy, I had hired a young Princeton graduate named Katie Mautner to be my assistant. I could see that she was whip-smart and driven; within a year she was a floor manager. Katie was more competent and hardworking than anyone I'd ever met, and she possessed a remarkably serene demeanor that put people around her at ease. Katie had a graduate degree from Cornell's School of Hotel Administration, and she had the backbone to push back when I was wrong, so one day I offered her the job of general manager at Craft. She was stunned and hesitated. "Trust me," I told her. "You can do this job." I wasn't wrong. Katie oversaw the entire construction project and managed the hiring process, all while planning her wedding to wine savant Paul Grieco, whom she had met at Gramercy.

As an aside: I've never met a man who responds to the offer of a major promotion with hesitation and self-doubt. In Katie's case, it was conscientiousness—she wouldn't take a job unless she thought she could deliver the goods. But I mention it here because it bears noting that the best hires of my life have all been women, usually the ones who are being underestimated in their current jobs, and every one of them has gone on to exceed my expectations. So women of the hospitality world, hear this: Your self-doubt is unwarranted. And you don't have to wait until someone offers it to you, either. If you see a big job you want, go get it; chances are you're more than ready.

As the front of house at Craft began to take shape, I began to build the kitchen, which was located down a flight of steep stairs. The kitchen was a subterranean space, much smaller than Gramercy's, but we maximized it for efficiency. Once again, I was lucky enough to attract a dream team: Marco Canora, who had been one of my sous-chefs at Gramercy, became Craft's chef de cuisine. Years before, when I first hired him as a cook, Marco had been a long-haired biker from San Francisco. Now he was a soulful and accomplished chef who had spent summers running his mother's acclaimed Tuscany Inn in Edgartown on Martha's Vineyard. Jonathan Benno and James Tracey

With Marco Canora and Katie (Mautner) Grieco, 2002

were sous-chefs. Rock stars like Damon Wise, Akhtar Nawab, and Bill Knapp, who had all passed through Gramercy, as well as the great Karen DeMasco, a protégé of Claudia's on pastry, rounded out the murderer's row. Even David Chang got in on the action, starting as a reservationist and making his way into the kitchen as gardemanger. Everyone brought the same high level of creativity and skill that had made working at Gramercy so fun, but now they all thrilled to this new stripped-back concept—tempering our wilder instincts and channeling them in pursuit of mind-bending flavor. Like all great cooks, they understood that simple rarely means easier—in fact, it can be a lot more difficult. With nothing to hide behind, mistakes are immediately visible, so it had better be right. We hovered over our pans like helicopter parents, since being off by even a few seconds could ruin a dish. Half the battle was sourcing—I hunted down ingredients like milk-fed poulardes from Four Story Hill Farm, incandescent lamb from Elysian Fields, fish unloaded directly from dayboat fishermen, diver-harvested scallops, and produce at peak season from the best local farms in the tri-state area. The product cost us an arm and a leg, but it made sense because each ingredient was essentially the star of its own show. You'd pay extra to see a star perform, right? Just as they had been at Lou Mazuc, the vegetables at Craft quickly became our calling card: our heirloom Nantes Coreless carrots, our puree of potatoes, the roasted hen of the woods mushrooms (these were the clear fan favorite; there was hell to pay if we ran out).

Working alongside my chefs as we bent over each piece of roasted fish or handful of wild mushrooms to coax out peak flavor, I realized we were putting aside our artistry and applying ourselves single-mindedly to our craft. If we did it exactly right—with no room for error—then that fish or those mushrooms or whatever else we were working with would taste profoundly and exquisitely just like themselves, and any embellishment would not be missed. And that's why I called the place Craft.

I wrote the menu in keeping with the overall approach, weary of the voluble lyricism of fancy menus. We kept it simple—in retrospect, maybe a bit too simple. Similar to a steakhouse, diners would be free to choose the components of their meal—proteins, grains, mushrooms, vegetables, potatoes—at will, and it would all be served family-style to encourage sharing. To me the menu seemed easy enough, but I still had my doubts. This flew in the face of fine-dining norms. Would the public get it? Would they misinterpret the simplicity and feel short-changed? New Yorkers were used to plated food; would they feel comfortable diving in communally at a high-end restaurant? I briefly considered introducing French service. At Gramercy one day, I ran the idea by Danny, whose keen sense of hospitality I never stopped trusting. "Remember when we were in Italy together? That's the way we ate, and it was great," he insisted. "Just put the food on the table. People will get it."

Craft opened in March 2001. We were mobbed. New Yorkers were curious to see what I was up to on my own, and the novel concept generated a ton of press—not all of it flattering—though the food was winning us fans. I no longer worried, as I had when we opened Gramercy, that I might not live up to expectations. I had a new set of worries—I was now the principal player in two major New York City restaurants and planned to stay hands-on in both. Could I balance the two places and meet my other obligations? Dante was now eight years old, Lori and I were planning our wedding for September, and I had just signed a contract to write my first book. I had a lot on my plate. One thing I knew: No amount of positive reaction to Craft would make up for a decline at Gramercy Tavern, whether real or perceived, so I resolved to spend as much time there as I possibly could. In fact, I spent Craft's opening night in the kitchen at Gramercy.

In those pre-influencer days, a restaurant lived or died by the number of stars it was awarded by the *New York Times*. On June 27, 2001, William Grimes granted us three stars, headlining the review "With Such Scallops, Who Needs Free Will?"—a reference to all the options on our menu. "Craft invites diners to take a trip," he began. "The destination is a simpler, cleaner, more honest America, a place where the corn is bright yellow, the bread exhales clouds of yeasty sweetness and the fish swim in water as pure as Évian. It's a vision of food heaven, a land of strong, pure flavors and back-to-basics cooking techniques." Grimes took us to task for the way we'd structured the menu, pointing out that by the end of a meal, diners were likely to experience decision fatigue:

> In the abstract, freedom of choice is desirable. But the arts, including the culinary arts, function more efficiently as dictatorships. Down with interactivity. Readers do not really want to decide what happens in the next chapter of a novel, and diners are happiest submitting to the iron will of a good chef.

Grimes concluded his review with this: "I don't know if cooking can be virtuous, but in this sinful city, I'm sure that Craft is on the side of the angels." The knowledge that he (and our guests) truly got what I had been going for filled me with an indescribable feeling. I took his words to heart and made the menu simpler to navigate.

Lori and I were set to be married at the Allen Farm in Chilmark, on Martha's Vineyard. Lori had spent summers there growing up, and the island had become special to us as a couple. A few days before the wedding, I traveled to the Vineyard for last-minute preparations (and peak fishing) and Lori flew to France to attend the Deauville

American Film Festival, where a film she'd directed was in competition. She called me with good news—her film had taken first prize, and she'd been invited to stay on an extra day to celebrate with friends in Paris. She passed on the party and left instead to join me—after all, we were getting married in five days, and there were still details to arrange. She landed late on September 10, 2001. Unbeknownst to us, she was on the last flight from Paris to Logan Airport in Boston before the attacks.

Early on September 11, I was on the water fishing with a captain who took an urgent phone call from his daughter in New York City. I watched him grow pale, then turn the boat around, tersely sharing what he'd learned. We docked, and I joined Lori and her sister in front of the TV, aghast at the footage of planes plowing into the World Trade Center, of buildings filled with people imploding downward in a torrent of thick gray debris. First came the calls to everyone and anyone we knew who had reason to be nearby. Kristen worked in the Financial District, and thankfully she and Dante, who had been in his Greenwich Village school when the planes hit, were fine. Bob Scott had been walking into the tower just as the first plane hit, but with the help of a former New York cop, he made his way out a side entrance in time. Through some miracle, no one in our immediate circle had died in the attacks, though, like all New Yorkers, we were but one or two degrees of separation from many who had, including Heather Ho, a former pastry cook at Gramercy Tavern, and Joe Mistrulli, a buoyant carpenter who had helped us build Craft and was working on the restoration of Windows on the World.

Our first impulse was to cancel the wedding. The world had ground to a halt: Craft's suppliers had all shut their operations, so there would be no food delivery for the reception. The nation's airports were closed, and our out-of-town guests had their flights canceled. And among those who could get there, who would want to celebrate in the midst of such heartbreak and devastation? Dancing, reveling in any way, felt unimaginable. Our rabbi, Bonnie Cohen, had arrived and pulled Lori and me aside. We told her we were considering canceling the wedding. Bonnie pointed to the words Lori had had inscribed inside my new wedding ring: "Don't Postpone Joy." The Torah, Bonnie explained, sees joy as the baseline human condition. It doesn't let you choose: Joy, no joy. *Feh*. If so much as one person wants to rejoice, then it is the world's obligation to rejoice with them.

And then the phone calls started. Friends as far away as Chicago had rented cars and were on their way. My chefs at Craft had started making calls and our suppliers were responding. Soon refrigerated trucks began showing up with everything we needed. By the next day, cars filled with loved ones were emptying out onto the lawn at the Allen Farm and people embraced tearfully. The sheer gratitude at seeing one another alive, healthy, breathing, was overwhelming. Lori and I looked at each other. Guess this thing was on.

The wedding itself was a blur, but the pictures tell a funny and touching story—shot after shot of my gruff New Jersey Italian aunts and uncles with their arms around Lori's kibitzy Jewish relatives. Two groups of people with very little in common discovered, after an unspeakable trauma, that they had everything in common, and everything to live for. And yes, people danced.

In lieu of a honeymoon, we returned immediately to the city and volunteered on one of the World Yacht boats harbored nearby to service Ground Zero. I cooked the midnight shift in the boat's galley kitchen, shoulder to shoulder with a Cantonese cook from Flushing and a couple of pizza guys from Bay Ridge. Lori poured coffee for shell-shocked ironworkers and machinists who could barely be persuaded to sleep for an hour or two before they headed back out into the fiery remains to continue their harrowing search for bodies.

I wish I could say that life soon returned to normal—it didn't, of course. There was a palpable sense of connection among strangers in those devastating weeks and months after the attacks. The entire city flinched with each low-flying plane. Flyers affixed to buildings with desperate pleas for missing loved ones eventually faded and frayed, but the sadness remained. When people began to dine out again, the simple authenticity of Craft's food seemed to resonate for a city desperate for comfort.

Danny and I stayed friendly but busied ourselves with separate projects. He had gone on to open Blue Smoke, a barbecue restaurant; the Modern, at the Museum of Modern Art; and the first Shake Shack kiosk in Madison Square Park. I was focused on Craft and Gramercy, but my world was expanding, too. In 2002 I had opened a casual cousin of Craft called Craftbar, next door on 19th Street, and a steakhouse iteration of Craft, named Craftsteak, in Las Vegas, followed by a line of sandwich shops called 'wichcraft in 2003. I had other projects in the works, and recently a TV producer had reached out about having me judge a reality cooking competition, which at the time sounded faintly ludicrous—who would want to watch a show about food they couldn't taste? My first book, *Think Like a Chef*, had won the James Beard Award for best cookbook, and a second book was in the works. Things were going well for both of us.

Around this time a group of Japanese investors became frequent visitors to Gramercy, eating there repeatedly over the course of a couple weeks—in the dining room, in the tavern, at the bar. I had twice been to Japan as part of a culinary delegation, and opening there would have been a dream project. Gramercy had a huge following in Japan, and I later learned these men had been making a fervent pitch to USHG to open a Gramercy Tavern in Tokyo, under excellent terms. They were steered to Union Square Cafe instead. There are two sides to every story, of course, but to me it felt as though Gramercy was once again being denied the growth it had richly earned. Partnerships are built on the trust that each party has the other's best interest in mind. When that trust ebbs, it's only a matter of time before the partnership runs aground.

Which is why, on the day Danny called me up with a proposition, I was open to it. He was looking to consolidate his business, and having one of his restaurants with outside ownership didn't fit his plan.

"I think either you should buy Gramercy from me, or I'll buy it from you," he said.

"Okay," I told him. "I'm not interested in selling, but I'll buy you out. What do you want for it?"

Danny threw out a number. It was high, the kind of number you give when you don't actually want to sell something but want credit for offering. I suggested instead that we bring in an accountant to go through the books and come up with a fair market valuation. So that's what we did. I took that number to Bob and my other investors at Craft, who were all in favor of the deal. Our lawyers began drawing up the paperwork.

My wish to keep Gramercy was knee-jerk and immediate. But then another thought began to nag at me. In its heyday, we had a dream team running Gramercy Tavern: Nick Mautone (the general manager), Claudia Fleming, Paul Grieco—all were now legends in their own right. They all had moved on, and while we still had a terrific team, I felt nostalgic for that earlier time. Ten years in, the restaurant was still reliably excellent, but the energy had changed, and I had changed, too.

Should I sell Gramercy Tavern to Danny, rather than buy it? My mother was dead set against the idea. "You're going to regret it, Tom. Maybe not now but in ten, twenty years, you'll wish Gramercy was still yours," she said. But it was already too late; that old familiar itch had returned, the piece of me that is always searching for the next new thing. I'd never be able to bring back the old crew, and it was time for me to look forward, not back. So instead of buying the place, I gave Danny a price to buy out my shares. He agreed, and that's how, in a matter of weeks, Gramercy Tavern was no longer mine. I'm happy to say we parted friends.

Soon after, Danny brought on the excellent Michael Anthony and the legend of Gramercy Tavern has only grown under his leadership. When I walk past those plate glass windows on 20th Street today, I feel a poignant sense of satisfaction, the way one does about a child who has grown up and moved out of the house. Though they're no longer in your care, you never really stop plugging for them and hoping they do well in the world.

10

Into the Future

FLASHBACK TO JUNE 1991: I was two months shy of thirty. Mondrian was a big hit with critics and diners, and I had just been awarded Best New Chef by *Food & Wine* magazine. To publicize the award, *Food & Wine* booked me on *Live! with Regis & Kathie Lee*. It was my first television appearance, and I was excited.

By way of context, I should share that I come from a long line of Elizabeth, New Jersey, TV lovers, which is to say the television played loud and proud all day every day in our house when I was growing up—we may have even left it on when we went to church. If I had to guess the moment when my mother really believed I'd made it, I'd put money on it *not* being when I first earned three stars in the *New York Times* or when I won my first James Beard Award. It was when I called her to say, "Ma, I'm going on *Regis & Kathie Lee*."

We were set to tape on a Monday morning, and, as instructed, I dutifully showed up for a quick run-through the Friday before. On my way out of the studio I stopped someone who appeared official and asked them what time I should get there for taping on Monday.

The guy looked at me. "Eight a.m.," he said, adding sternly, "Don't be late."

Monday morning I showed up with everything prepped and ready to go for a dish of braised red snapper with an eggplant napoleon and lemon rosemary vinaigrette, including a finished "swap out" for the big reveal at the end. I was met at the door by a screeching producer. "Where the f*$^ have you been? You were supposed to be here hours ago!!" The woman was apoplectic. "I've got him!" she barked into a walkie, yanking me toward the soundstage. I glanced down at my watch. It was exactly 8 a.m. I tripped along after her, clutching my mise en place while she continued to rail at me. "You know, you missed rehearsal!" she snapped. From the corner of my eye I glimpsed the guy I'd asked for instructions on Friday, standing in a small group of guys dressed just like him, all watching and laughing. His ID tag read "stagehand."

We set everything up in a flash, but I was rattled. All the clever things I had lined up to say flew clear out of my mind, and I made my way through the segment thoroughly freaked out. At one point Regis turned and gave the camera an elfin grin: "Guess that's what happens when you miss rehearsal!" I was mortified. Regis Philbin, the king of morning television and darling of soccer moms everywhere, had just thrown me under the bus. (Later I learned he'd been quipping about his own missed rehearsal.) No one seemed to notice. Regis and Kathie Lee helped themselves to bites of the finished dish, and as they cut away to commercial, the producer, a wholly changed person at this point, reappeared to shake my hand. "We'd love to have you back!" she chirped. Fat chance, I thought as I showed myself out. I'm never doing TV again.

As it turned out, I did plenty of cooking spots over the years. I grew adept at it and developed a rapport with many hosts and producers, grateful they were helping to keep my work in front of the public. Because the reality was, the vast majority of people in the country weren't going to experience my food in person, not even on a special occasion. I was cooking for the fortunate few, and the fact of that was starting to bother me more and more. Even Craftbar, the lower-priced neo-bistro we'd opened in 2002, was out of reach for the majority of New Yorkers, who were from working-class families like the one I had grown up in.

———

It had also been bothering me that the only sandwich worth getting out of bed for in New York City was all the way downtown on Sullivan Street, at a tiny grocery called Melampo Imported Foods, which was damn inconvenient as my offices were thirty blocks north, four floors above Craft. Melampo's owner, Alessandro Gualandi, was the most unabashedly grumpy human I'd ever laid eyes on, and it was worth the trip just to observe him in his natural habitat, a twelve-foot-wide storefront with one of two soundtracks playing: opera or Seton Hall basketball. Gualandi made people skittish with his rules, which actually boiled down to just two: *The line forms to the left and you better know what you want by the time you get up here*, and *no substitutions*. I'd grown up with uncles exactly like Gualandi, so I liked the guy. One day he looked up at me as I placed my order and asked, "You that guy Colicchio?" I nodded. Yes, I was. As the ever-growing line behind me watched, he took his time making me the single best sandwich of my life—prosciutto, capocollo, mortadella, bresaola, all imported or house-cured, and layered with mozzarella that had been hand-pulled that morning at Joe's Dairy across the street, adding a tablespoon or two of homemade giardiniera for bite, a drizzle of imported olive oil, and a hint of peperoncini, which were drying in bunches from the ceiling overhead. When it was the next guy's turn, he said, "I'll have what you made him, please," to which Gualandi replied, "No you won't. Get the hell outta my store."

In case you can't tell, I like sandwiches. At home I frequently twist off a heel of bread and wrap it around a few fingers of whatever we have—cheese, prosciutto, good jam—and that can be breakfast, lunch, a snack. The idea to open 'wichcraft came from wanting to satisfy my daily itch for a sandwich coupled with the wish to offer really good food at a price point that would be accessible to more people. I partnered up to develop the menu with a young chef, Sisha Ortuzar, who had been doing great work for me, first at Gramercy and now at Craft. Our motto was "Craft between two pieces of bread." We cured our own meats, hand-made our condiments, and created a sandwich menu so good I think about it still. We opened 'wichcraft next door to Craftbar on 19th Street in the summer of 2003, and despite a

---

busted air conditioner during a record-hot summer, people formed a line out the door to come and eat our sandwiches. The place was a hit. Craftbar was also doing well. And in Las Vegas, Craftsteak had opened in the MGM Grand to raves from food lovers and gambling pensioners alike.

Which is why when offers started rolling in to replicate these successes, I said yes. And yes. And yes. We opened additional 'wichcrafts throughout Manhattan, along with a commissary on the far west side of Chelsea. Crafts Vegas, Dallas, Los Angeles, and Atlanta were all excellent restaurants in their own right, run by some of the most talented people their cities had on offer, but each in turn faltered through some combination of bad luck, bad location, or both. Craft Dallas was a perfect example: We had been approached by Dallas businessmen Ross Perot Jr. and Tom Hicks, who wanted Craft to be the capstone restaurant in a W hotel across from the new American Airlines Center, in a development that would eventually include the Mandarin Oriental and a host of luxury retail shops and condos. Peter Bentel designed a space that borrowed from the original Craft's DNA but engaged architecturally with Dallas's sprawling spatial optimism and sunshine. But when the larger development fell victim to the 2008 financial crisis, the Mandarin never opened, the condos went unbuilt, and Craft Dallas closed soon after.

If I'm really being honest with myself, there was something else at play other than the faltering economy. I had always prided myself on being both a chef and a businessman. But as the idea of Craft caught on, the pendulum swung away from my creative, evolving brain to the deal-making, entrepreneurial side. As these deals appeared, I leaped on them for the same reason that nine-year-old me sold cans of soda at the Feast of St. Rocco back in Elizabeth: because I could, a far cry from diving into a project from a place of curiosity and a desire to evolve creatively. At Craft we were still working intently to make the most flavorful and perfectly executed food in the world, but without Gramercy, I no longer had the kitchen that had been my culinary playground and laboratory for years, and I missed the process of experimentation and growth that it had afforded me.

I found myself leafing through my old books, as well as a host of newer titles on baking and fermentation that I'd added to my collection—the chemistry interested me. By now I was the head judge on Bravo's *Top Chef*, and I was being exposed to an array of chefs whose use of their own families' food traditions in their work were broadening my own education. I wanted to learn more about different culinary foodways, about the intersection of food with culture and history. I started spending time in markets like Kalustyan's in Manhattan's Kips Bay, a dazzling bazaar of South Asian spices, condiments, and specialty foods. More than ever, I was becoming aware of the way in which our industry's bias toward "classical" (code for European) training had constrained my own culinary imagination. I had no interest in trying to appropriate a cuisine that wasn't my own, but I began experimenting with chiles and spices like long pepper, which is fruitier than the traditional black pepper I knew, and berbere, the spice blend of North African nomadic tribes with an intriguing mixture of heat, spice, and citrus. At times I played with just a daub of these spices on the side of the plate, so that their complex aroma would cause an olfactory intersection with the flavors of the dish.

This new surge of creative inquiry culminated in a weekly pop-up called Tom's Tuesday Dinners, which we served from Craft's private dining space one night a week. (Why Tuesday? Why not?) I designed a menu that integrated these new influences into the plated and complex style of cooking from my Gramercy Tavern years. With two chefs alongside me, I cooked in an open kitchen, turning out dishes like squab with vadouvan, a masala blend merging traditional Indian spices with fennel, mace, and shallots, and squid stuffed with chorizo and kale served with a cocoa nib and chili sauce. We put out the word among Craft's fans and kept it small—only thirty or so covers a night.

The reception to Tom's Tuesday Dinners was overwhelmingly positive, and inside I knew why: I was learning and creating again, and excited about it, and while Lori would not describe self-awareness as my crowning strength, I was starting to realize just how important it was that I keep growing, both for the health of my business and for my own personal evolution.

And there was something else that aided that evolution: I became a father for the second time. Luka Bodhi Colicchio was born on August 1, 2009, with a full head of hair and huge blue eyes that took in the world around him with wonder from the very first second he was hatched. Luka was the toddler who said hi to every stranger on the subway and bent to examine each blade of grass, experiencing it as exactly the miracle it was (walking a block with the kid could take an hour or more). Luka's natural state was one of empathy and joy, which persists to this day, despite his best efforts to emulate a moody teenager.

Nineteen months after Luka was born, on March 22, 2011, Mateo Lev Colicchio arrived. Mateo spent the first week of his life in the NICU recovering from a lung infection. Sitting beside his incubator brought me back emotionally to Dante's infancy. Mateo weighed a hearty seven pounds when he was born; some of the babies alongside us weighed two pounds or less. We knew how lucky we were to go home with a healthy infant after just one week, while others would clearly be there for many weeks and even months.

Mateo instantly asserted his role in our household as its fiercest and most determined member. He pulled himself to standing at five months and was walking at nine months, which sounds like bragging but isn't. We were now running after two drunken sailor-anarchists with the insatiable need to touch, feel, and taste everything they could reach. Mateo soon began to beat me at my best game: arguing. Luckily for us (and the world), his scrappiness was balanced by a strong sense of fairness and compassion. The boys were different in almost every way but one: their unshakeable belief that Dante, now a teenager, was God.

I was an older father this time around and had the time and freedom to bond with Luka and Mateo, much as I had had with baby Dante during those months before Gramercy Tavern's opening, but this precious time was punctuated by long absences while shooting *Top Chef*. The shoots, typically lasting weeks at a time over late summer and fall, were hard on our young family. Thankfully, we had the help of Tenzin Kunsang, a kind and soulful young woman who cared for the kids while we worked. Over the eight years she was with us, Tenzin grew to know and love Luka and Mateo like they were her own.

Top Chef was now a major part of my career, though it had begun inauspiciously enough five years before with a phone call from a television producer named Shauna Minoprio, who worked for an LA production company called Magical Elves. "We're doing a reality show for Bravo," she had said after introducing herself. "It's like *Project Runway* but with food. We think you'd be great." I wasn't terribly interested. For one thing, Lori, a film snob, was dead set against the idea. I had won five James Beard Awards, she argued. Why chip away at that prestige by diving into reality competition? This was a TV genre that, in the mid-2000s, was still unmistakably cheesy—think shows like *Big Brother* and *Survivor*. The producers asked me to travel to Los Angeles for a screen test. I told them that if they wanted to see me on-screen, there were dozens of clips out there of me doing stand-and-stir routines on morning shows, as well as a documentary about the opening of Craft that had been produced by ABC News. They took a look at the documentary and came back with an offer. I was still only lukewarm on the idea. Magical Elves was persistent, though, and sent me two stacks of *Project Runway* DVDs (this was long before streaming). The show, which they also produced, had just ended its second season.

Lori, Dante, and I ordered in some takeout and started watching *Project Runway* on a Friday night. Come Sunday the three of us were still in our pajamas, empty pizza boxes and snack wrappers littering the room, as we watched the final episode of season two, wishing we could start on a third. We didn't know it, but we had just had our first experience of binge-watching. *Project Runway* felt different from the silly competition shows that had come before: There was a documentary quality and an emphasis on process that lent seriousness and intrigue to the pursuit of success in fashion, an industry that was unknown to me until then. The high production value tipped the scales for me, and I decided to go for it, reasoning that a show that gave viewers that same kind of inside baseball for the food world could be a great thing for the restaurant industry. Even better, I felt it could impact our country as eaters. As I was learning from my growing advocacy work, far too many people didn't understand where our food came from or took for granted the backbreaking hard work, skill, and thought that went into producing it. I thought *Top Chef* might have a hand in changing that.

So I agreed to do the show on one condition: The judges would have the final decision over who stayed, who left, and who won. I wanted this show to be taken seriously by my colleagues in the industry. Chefs have a keen sense of smell and can detect bullshit even through the tubes of their TVs.

I arrived for our first shoot in San Francisco in the summer of 2006. Being on a television show might sound glamorous, but the making of it—at least at this level—was decidedly not. The production was operating on a shoestring and had booked the opening cast—myself, Gail Simmons (soon to become one of my favorite people of all time), and the affable Katie Lee Joel—into a hotel called the Diva, in the Tenderloin district. Though the hotel looked fine in pictures, it turned out to be a bleak flophouse with fraying sheets, a soiled comforter, and aromatic carpet dating from the days of disco. The rooms were rentable by the hour. This was to be my home for the next month? I called Lori to complain. "Stop bellyaching," she told me. "You're being a spoiled brat." When she arrived for a visit a week later, she took a quick look around the room (easily done, as it was the size of the bed) and reached for her phone. "Pack your stuff," she instructed me. "We're leaving." This from a woman who had lived in shanty-towns for her own work. We decamped for a better hotel nearby. (I later learned that the Diva was converted to supportive housing.)

The pacing of television production was new to me; there was a lot of hurry up and wait as complicated camera and lighting rigs were assembled and disassembled on set. (This was actually an advantage, as it gave me plenty of downtime to work remotely with my teams at Gramercy Tavern and Craft.) The logistics of producing food in a variety of settings tested the *Top Chef* crew, as did mistakes like casting for "personality" over culinary skill. Early seasons shone a light on the casual misogyny that was still so rampant in our industry in the 2000s. We judges spent little time with the chefs during competition, so we never saw it until we watched the completed episodes. It was jarring to see the difference between some of the male contestants' polite deference to us and their locker-room comments or off-hand disrespect toward the women competing alongside them.

Top Chef debuted to decent ratings. It seemed as though people wanted to know more about food and the people who pursued a life in it. With each successive season, we got better at making the show, and I became an executive producer so I could have a hand in its creative direction. We realized the value in bringing on a dedicated culinary producer,

such as former contestant Lee Anne Wong, whose unique firsthand experience on the show translated into smarter decisions and smoother shoots. Our budget thankfully grew (these days they put me up in a comfortable Airbnb while shooting), and we branched out internationally, first for our finales, and eventually for the entire twentieth season, which was shot in London and Paris. Most importantly, the

At judges' table with Joe Flamm, Kristen Kish, and Gail Simmons

producers came to trust that the cooking itself created the drama so we didn't need to fall into the traps of other reality shows. I learned that a television show is not unlike a new restaurant—it can take a few seasons to iron out the kinks.

Though *Top Chef* raised my public profile, it took up only eight weeks out of my year, and the remaining forty-four (minus the fishing) were focused on my real work in restaurants. One night a diner approached me after her meal at a Tuesday Dinner: "I had no idea you could cook like this!" she enthused. That threw me for a loop. Any chef who says they don't read online reviews from their diners is full of it; of course we do. I was noticing a trend among people who wrote in after their meals at Craft: They praised the food lavishly but showed surprise that it was all so simple. After all, they'd come to Craft expressly to experience the work of the Great Judger of Food on Television, who critiqued complex dishes on the show. So when our restaurant Craftsteak in the Meatpacking District was faltering, I told my partners I wanted to invest in a redesign of the space. Tom's Tuesday Dinners had gotten my creative juices flowing, and I was ready to plunge back into the kind of intricate and highly personal cooking that had built my career.

By now I was the father of sons—plural—and when Lori threw out the name Colicchio & Sons, she meant it as a joke, but I liked it. My sons represented newness and excitement to me, and that was precisely how I was feeling about the food I was now creating. My chef de cuisine in this new venture was Damon Wise, a rock-solid and immensely talented chef who had come to me from Lespinasse and been my right hand for years as we opened Crafts around the country. Stephen Collucci, recently the head of pastry at our flagship Craft, began turning out mind-bending desserts. I built upon and outward from what I had been doing at Tom's Tuesday Dinners and took risks, like layering lamb with caramelized yogurt or juxtaposing dishes from my past to form new ones, like foie gras terrine with one single perfect Craft-inspired scallop. I was cooking for guests, obviously, but I was also cooking for myself. How and what could I cook to keep myself interested?

When the *New York Times* review for Colicchio & Sons came out in 2010, Sam Sifton gave us three stars, and he seemed to fully grasp my expanding worldview, writing,

> There are elements of French technique to the cooking here, as well as an appreciable Italian devotion to ingredients. There are Indian flavors, and central European ones; there are nods also at Spain, at the Greenmarket, at North Africa. The result is a menu with an aesthetic that is entirely American.

That year, I received the James Beard Award for Outstanding Chef, an award reserved for a chef who has already received the top award in their respective region (I had won Best Chef in New York in 2000).

With the increased visibility of *Top Chef* came increased opportunities to do things I cared about. I had long been involved in the fight against hunger with Share Our Strength, now called No Kid Hungry, and I admired the way the organization was working intelligently, state by state, to remove legislative and bureaucratic obstacles to kids getting fed. I cooked at galas and fundraisers for them and other anti-hunger groups like Food Bank for New York City, City Harvest, and Bread for the World to try to raise awareness and funds. Like many people, I assumed that was the best way to help.

Around this time Lori began to mentor a little girl named Sabrina who lived in an East Harlem shelter, helping her with homework or just lending an ear. The shelter where Sabrina lived was rat-infested and dehumanizing. Sabrina's mother was frequently hospitalized, leaving Sabrina and her siblings in the care of overwhelmed relatives. When Lori brought Sabrina over to our place, I'd offer to make her anything she liked. She always asked for the same thing: salad. Sabrina found all fresh fruits and vegetables exotic. They were rare and precious to her. She ate the first peach of her life on our porch one day and stared at us in shock, amazed that something could taste that damn good, and so we filled a sack full of them to bring back to her siblings at home. In fact, we pressed bags of food on Sabrina every chance we got. We knew that her family subsisted on the cheapest food available: ramen noodles and chips, with the occasional fast-food meal split among the siblings as a treat. Even with the help of food stamps, these foods made up the bulk of Sabrina's diet.

We were able to help Sabrina get into a small school for kids with learning differences, where she began to display mystifying behaviors. Despite her usual good nature, she'd lapse into fits of implacable anger. She would put her head down on her desk and sleep for hours, unrousable. She was frequently sick, suffering persistent colds and serious infections. Her teeth were a constant source of pain, showing early signs of decay; one even fell out, and it wasn't a baby tooth. And then one day we got a call from the school's principal: Sabrina had been rummaging in the garbage for food. In fact, he explained, most days he or a teacher would share with her the food they had brought in for themselves from home, as the school was too small for a cafeteria, and kids who went there brought in their own lunch. That's when we connected the dots: Sabrina was hungry. Not just every so often, but frequently, relentlessly. It was interfering with her mood, her ability to learn, and her self-esteem. Once she asked Lori, "How come other kids get to eat?"

By now Lori's short films had earned her Hollywood agents, and her first feature-length fiction film, *On the Outs*, co-directed with Michael Skolnik, was a critical success. Studio jobs had begun rolling in. But here was a more urgent story that needed telling. How could it be that less than a mile away from New York City's highest temples of elite cuisine, children like Sabrina were literally losing the teeth in their head from hunger? How could it be that in the wealthiest nation on Earth, a country literally awash in food, we had millions of undernourished children? With all the record-breaking money we were raising for charity, why was the problem growing worse with each passing year?

And that is how I suddenly found myself the executive producer of *A Place at the Table*, a documentary film co-directed by Lori and her highly regarded partner, filmmaker Kristi Jacobson, that followed three everyday hardworking Americans whose families were battling food insecurity. Lori and Kristi weren't interested in "poverty porn," as they called the genre of films that gave viewers a vicarious view of suffering. They wanted to make a movie that would spell out the solutions and then use it to hold our leaders accountable.

For once we could exploit my celebrity for something other than making dinner reservations. We arranged to have me address a meeting of the congressional Committee on Education and the Workforce at the Capitol in Washington, DC, while Lori and Kristi filmed (members of Congress, curiously, are really into *Top Chef*). The meeting was to discuss Congress's plan to cut funding for school meals, which was on the chopping block along with almost all programs for struggling Americans in 2010. These were a casualty of the Bush tax cuts, which accrued disproportionately to the top 1 percent of earners, while close to fifty million Americans were finding it hard to afford basic nutrition after the Great Recession. The thesis of *A Place at the Table* was clear: We had more than enough food to feed everyone in America healthfully and well, but a series of poor policy decisions was keeping us from doing it. A handful of politicians were cynically leading the charge to cut food assistance, exploiting racist and discredited tropes about welfare queens and food stamp fraud. We had solved this vexing problem back in the 1970s through a series of smart policies and programs that made food available widely and cheaply for all, but

from the 1980s onward, we had flipped our national priorities, and it was time to demand that our elected officials make ending hunger a priority again.

A Place at the Table debuted at Sundance in 2013. Almost overnight, my scene in the film where I confronted Congress seemed to change the media's perception of me, and therefore the public's. I was no longer "that TV chef," or maybe more precisely, I was still "that TV chef" but now one who was also enlisted to speak out on how we could end hunger in this country. Appearances on serious news programs gave me a platform to talk about other issues that mattered to me, like the importance of supporting our farmers and sustainable agriculture, the labeling of GMOs, and the health of our oceans.

I'm very proud of the work this new prominence allowed me to do. Together with Ken Cook and Scott Faber of the Environmental Working Group, I helped create a group called Food Policy Action, which was designed to expose our elected officials' voting records on issues pertaining to food. At first members of Congress dismissed the idea—voters didn't care about food issues, they told us—but once we started issuing and publicizing a report card grading them for how they voted on things like ending hunger, supporting the rights and dignity of farm and food workers, and protecting and maintaining sustainable fisheries, they changed their tune. I began showing up for lobbying days, making the rounds of politicians to advocate for better food policies. Soon the James Beard Foundation started training other chefs to lobby, so we'd show up as a delegation to talk to members of Congress. I recalled my father in his union organizing days, and how proud he was to "stand up for the little guy," as he described it, and I felt lucky to have a platform to do it myself.

Here's what I'm less proud of: My ego fed, ravenously, on all of it. I was now being ushered ahead to the front of lines, asked to pose on red carpets, being given lifts on private airplanes. Lori and I started getting invited annually to the Vanity Fair Oscar Party, where movie stars would mob me with cooking questions (I'd never met skinnier people so obsessed with food) and request to appear on *Top Chef*. The show has hosted an amazing array of guest judges, including Natalie

Portman (my favorite), Ali Wong, Kate Winslet, Charlize Theron, Patti LaBelle, Jennifer Coolidge, Aisha Tyler, Penn & Teller, Lorraine Bracco, Chris Pratt, Anna Faris . . . the list goes on and on, and I would be lying if I said I didn't enjoy my newfound proximity to all of them. I was invited to appear on the Super Bowl pregame show. I was on the receiving end of frequent awards. I lapped up the attention.

What I missed, though, through the lens of my spectacular self-regard, was that two of the people I loved most in the world were not doing so well. Dante, who had left college early in his sophomore year, was struggling with anxiety and depression, and though his mother and Lori tried to raise alarm bells with me about it, I brushed them off. Today I understand this pattern in myself—when I'm scared or don't have solutions, I go into denial or become defensive—but back then I simply said something brilliant like "all kids go through stuff" and left them to try to figure out how to support him on their own. Lori began to crumble under the pressure of raising our kids with an oft-absent spouse while also trying to keep up with her demanding career. Rather than help more, I continued to say yes to every appearance and opportunity, sulking that she, a working mother of two kids under three, wasn't as keen on playing dress-up and coming along as my personal cheerleader.

Both of our boys were now showing clear signs of ADHD and needed the extra energy and support that comes with that. Staying consistent with my pattern when I'm afraid, I did nothing, disregarding Lori's exhaustion and leaving her to handle it as competently as she had handled everything else for our kids that required research and attention. I'm ashamed to say that I processed her burnout, which soon turned into major depression, as a giant drag for me and even made her feel bad about herself; where had my fun playmate gone? Lori suggested couples counseling, but I was uninterested; she was the one with the problem, so if she wanted to get therapy, fine, but leave me out of it. After all, I didn't drink, gamble, or run around with other women. I was a good provider. To my mind, I was doing everything right, or at least doing everything differently than my father had.

Or was I?

Lori began to pull away. And then something terrifying happened: That summer, when I left to shoot *Top Chef*, she realized that she didn't miss me. Life for her as a working mother with two rambunctious and demanding boys, a household to run, a needy dog, and a full calendar of work and high-level activism was actually easier and better without me than with me. She was done.

We started counseling the week I returned.

Lori had already been in therapy and had an easier time with the process; I argued way more than I listened. I railed and harrumphed my way through the first year or so, preferring to make my point rather than make a connection. The truth is I was terrified. The work was requiring a level of self-honesty and vulnerability I had never attempted before. But little by little, I started to understand myself better and came to see the role my own conditioning around manhood had played in the breakdown of the single best thing that had ever happened to me.

A few things prodded me along. First was the #MeToo movement. I felt good about never having tolerated harassment in any of my restaurants. But the voices of the women in our industry were prominent now in a way they had never been before; it forced me to listen in a deeper and more active way in order to understand the thousands of invisible obstacles to success that women still faced— from shrinking reproductive rights to being expected to remember all the family birthdays and doctor's appointments—that most men never have to worry about during their most productive career years. I couldn't help but see the parallels in my own life, the sacrifices Lori was expected to make so I could have it all. I had been lucky enough to grow up watching a father who, for all his faults, treated women with respect. That had been my model. But while I have not sexually harassed anyone, I realized I was nonetheless operating within the same toxic tropes of male infallibility that had hurt generations of women, and, more specifically, the one in my own home. What was this teaching our sons? How would this serve them in their own relationships one day?

Another thing that forced me to grow was the pandemic. In March 2020, Lori and I and the boys moved to our farmhouse on

Long Island's North Fork, joined at times by Dante (who was back in school and doing much better) and his girlfriend Alex. Suddenly I was a man with a lot of time on his hands. No more galas. No more red carpets. No more *Top Chef.* Any media hits I was doing were for the unglamorous purpose of talking about how to help our industry survive, and they happened over a laptop propped up on a stack of my kids' books. My restaurants were all closed. I had no idea if they would ever reopen. Letting go of the three-hundred-plus people who worked for me in one fell swoop was unquestionably the worst day of my career. Like so many people, I was now living in a space of terrifying uncertainty that bordered on the existential: If I wasn't a chef, what—or more importantly *who*—was I, exactly?

And if the family I loved was falling apart, what did any of it even matter?

When our country shut down in March 2020, the restaurant industry went dark overnight, plunging millions of restaurant and restaurant-adjacent workers into peril. I was part of a group of chefs who banded together to look for ways to help our industry and the people working within it survive. Up until this point there was no confederation or organization representing the tens of thousands of independent restaurants in the United States. There was something called the National Restaurant Association that purported to speak for chain and fast-food workers, but they hardly counted as advocates; the last time they'd banded together for anything, it was to screw their employees out of fairer wages.

Thanks to some foundation money that got us started, we created the Independent Restaurant Coalition, or IRC, and set to work recruiting every single independent restaurant, from the fanciest high temples of gastronomy to the smallest mom-and-pop cafés, to come together and speak with one voice, asking to be included in the American Rescue Plan. Independent restaurants like ours represented close to $11 billion in the US economy, and if we went under, that loss would have a devastating cascade of effects on all the businesses that relied upon us for survival, like growers and fisheries and truckers and laundries and beverage distributors and so many more.

Word traveled fast and the IRC began holding daily 10 a.m. Zoom calls—first with just a dozen or so participants, eventually with many hundreds—to strategize and connect small restaurant owners with support. There are too many people who were instrumental in making it happen to list here, but after nearly a year of the IRC's intensive lobbying, the Restaurant Revitalization Fund was passed by Congress in April 2022, allocating $28.6 billion in relief funds, which provided a lifeline to thousands of restaurants, starting with BIPOC- and women-owned businesses, as they had been hardest hit by the pandemic. After years of being the center of attention, here was something I couldn't have pulled off without hundreds of my peers. It was humbling. It was also the high point of my career. The bill was cosponsored by Representative Earl Blumenauer of Oregon and Senator Roger Wicker of Mississippi. Most importantly, thousands of independent restaurateurs who had maybe once considered themselves lone actors now understood they were part of a group that could stand together and have a voice in our democracy.

Around this time, I also started doing cooking demonstrations over Zoom. One of the questions I was asked most frequently was "Why do you cook?"

Good question.

It got me thinking, mostly of my grandfather. On the nights before he and I would go crabbing in Barnegat Bay, I'd sleep over at his house and wake up before dawn to the smell of frying peppers and onions. He cooked so we'd have something to eat out on the water.

The crabs we caught would come home in a sack, and I would clean them and my grandmother would start making a crab gravy that took hours and was the most delicious thing on Earth. One by one, drawn by the smell, my family would start to gather, this one dragging a bit of bread through the pot to taste, that one pulling up a chair, until eventually we were all sitting down together. Soon aunts, uncles, and cousins would show up, and they'd sit down, too. Everyone had their own particular method for picking and eating crab; it was a topic of much debate. As was everything else under the sun: We debated politics and sports and television shows and *can you believe the gas prices?* We discussed whose kids were doing what, and who was cheating on who, and there was ribbing and there was laughter, uproarious laughter, because *get outta here* if you can't take a joke. That was why my family cooked—because it gave us a reason to all sit around and be together. That was what I loved about it. That was why I had started cooking; I loved how it connected us, and once I discovered I had a knack for it and could make my family happy by doing it, I wanted to do it even more.

So now, at the hardest and most uncertain time of my life, that's what I did. I started to cook, just for the four of us. Most of the recipes in this book are the food I made during that time, a collection of the kinds of things I've always liked to cook at home. I also started baking bread (then again, who didn't?). But mostly, I became a stay-at-home dad. Taking care of my family's most basic needs became my job. I got my shit in order and started shouldering more of the grunt work of running our family.

Lori and I started to rebuild. I worked to hold space for her and her work by managing what I could of our lives and her creative work began to flourish. As of this writing, she likes me again.

A number of my restaurants, including Riverpark and our 'wichcrafts, closed permanently during the pandemic. Others we brought back little by little as regulations governing indoor businesses rolled back. I have not yet given up on making the perfect sandwich (stay tuned for more on this), but despite the world being in terrible turmoil as I write this, despite climate change and the clear and present threats to our democracy, I have reasons for optimism. A lot of it.

Why? For one thing, our industry has never been more equitable and attuned to the vast range of experiences, stories, and flavors that go into making great cuisine. We have never worked more effectively together to do so many good things—like fight hunger, poverty, and abuse. We have made space for people who don't look like me to become the next generation of stars. As a culture, we are rewriting the code for what it means to be strong, which demands resilience and openness, rather than brawn and posturing. We've called bullshit on tired old tropes of male chef-dom and made the mental health of our community a priority. And if you don't believe me, just take a look at the new generation of chefs who are somehow managing to create incredible food while staying present for their families, communities, and planet.

Incredible opportunities continue to come my way, but these days I feel confident enough to be discerning about the projects I choose—unless a proposal excites me creatively, I'm not interested. My definition of success has grown beyond James Beard Awards and stars in the *New York Times* to include the health of my relationships, both with my loved ones and with the people I am blessed to work with. I'm still working closely with my chefs in the restaurants, but I'm no longer on the pass at night, mostly because I want to eat dinner with my kids, and also because my knees and my back just don't like it.

I am cooking, though, maybe more than I ever have. We're blessed with a cohort of close family and friends (they know who they are) and I find my greatest pleasure is cooking for that crowd. It never gets old.

I like to play guitar and sing along. One of my favorite songs in the world is "Genesis" by Jorma Kaukonen, and as I draw this book to a close, the lyrics come to mind.

> *Time's come for us to pause*
> *And think of living as it was*
> *Into the future we must cross, must cross*
> *I'd like to go with you*
> *And I'd like to go with you*
>
> *You say I'm harder than a wall*
> *A marble shaft about to fall*
> *I love you dearer than them all, them all*
> *So let me stay with you*
> *So let me stay with you*

I think I'll end there.

Acknowledgments

I would like to thank Joshua David Stein.

Thank you to my entire team at Artisan—Lia Ronnen, Judy Pray, Brooke Beckmann, Suet Chong, Allison McGeehon, Cindy Lee, Zach Greenwald, Hillary Leary, and Nancy Murray, and to Suzanne Gluck at WME.

Thank you to Evan Sung and the food stylists—Dayna Seman, Cindy DiPrima, Alexandra Massillon, and Tea DiPrima—for your incredible artistry and professionalism. Thank you to Lauryn Tyrell for testing the recipes.

Thank you to Made In for their cookware. It is so good, I would actually pay for it, but thank you.

Thank you to my partners Bob Scott, Tom Tuft, Joe Wender, Ann Colgin, Katie Grieco, and Jeanne Donovan Fisher for your support all those years ago and to this day.

Thank you to every single member of my teams at Craft, Temple Court, Small Batch, Vallata, and Craftsteak Las Vegas for your incredible kindness, intelligence, and work ethic. You make me look good every day.

Thank you to Maya Land and everyone at Crafted Hospitality for making what I do possible, and demonstrating daily the care and humanity that we strive for as a company and as members of this industry.

Thank you to my family, especially my brothers, Michael and Phil, who have always been my biggest fans and helped make me who I am. Thank you to Phil Colicchio for always having my back. Thank you to my children, Dante, Luka, and Mateo, for being my best teachers and greatest inspiration.

Thank you to my mother, for whom there are not enough words of gratitude and love.

And thank you most of all to Lori, my partner in life, who has contributed immeasurably to my success. Love you to the moon and back.

Index

Page numbers in *italics* refer to recipe photos.

TOM COLICCHIO is an eight-time James Beard Award–winning chef and the owner of Crafted Hospitality, which includes New York City's Craft, Temple Court, and Vallata; Las Vegas's Craftsteak; and Small Batch in Garden City, New York. Born in Elizabeth, New Jersey, Tom made his New York cooking debut at prominent restaurants including the Quilted Giraffe, Gotham Bar & Grill, and Gramercy Tavern before opening Craft in 2001.

A vocal and outspoken social justice advocate, Tom executive-produced the 2013 documentary *A Place at the Table* about the underlying causes of hunger in the United States. This eye-opening experience led Tom on a journey to Washington, DC, where he has been a mainstay in our nation's capital in the years since. From holding members of Congress accountable on their voting records around food to working with former FLOTUS Michelle Obama on the Healthy, Hunger-Free Kids Act, Tom has established himself as the leading "Citizen Chef," advocating for a food system that values access, affordability, and nutrition over corporate interests.

Tom is a frequent contributor on several television shows and networks, including MSNBC, CNN, ABC, and Bloomberg, and is the host of the iHeart Radio podcast *Citizen Chef*. Tom is the head judge and executive producer of the Emmy-winning Bravo hit series *Top Chef*. He is the host and executive producer of a new interactive cooking show, *The Pantry*, on Spirits Network.

Tom lives in Brooklyn with his wife and their three sons. When not in the kitchen, Tom can be found tending his North Fork, Long Island, garden, fishing, or playing guitar.

Conversion Chart

For reference or general cooking, here are rounded-off equivalents between the metric system and the traditional systems that are used in the United States to measure weight and volume.

WEIGHTS

US/UK	METRIC
1 oz	30 g
2 oz	55 g
3 oz	85 g
4 oz (¼ lb)	115 g
5 oz	140 g
6 oz	170 g
7 oz	200 g
8 oz (½ lb)	225 g
9 oz	255 g
10 oz	285 g
11 oz	310 g
12 oz	340 g
13 oz	370 g
14 oz	395 g
15 oz	425 g
16 oz (1 lb)	455 g

VOLUME

AMERICAN	IMPERIAL	METRIC
¼ tsp		1.25 ml
½ tsp		2.5 ml
1 tsp		5 ml
½ Tbsp (1½ tsp)		7.5 ml
1 Tbsp (3 tsp)		15 ml
¼ cup (4 Tbsp)	2 fl oz	60 ml
⅓ cup (5 Tbsp)	2½ fl oz	75 ml
½ cup (8 Tbsp)	4 fl oz	125 ml
⅔ cup (10 Tbsp)	5 fl oz	150 ml
¾ cup (12 Tbsp)	6 fl oz	175 ml
1 cup (16 Tbsp)	8 fl oz	250 ml
1¼ cups	10 fl oz	300 ml
1½ cups	12 fl oz	350 ml
2 cups (1 pint)	16 fl oz	500 ml
2½ cups	20 fl oz (1 pint)	625 ml
5 cups	40 fl oz (1 qt)	1.25 l

OVEN TEMPERATURES

	°F	°C	GAS MARK
very cool	250–275	130–140	½–1
cool	300	148	2
warm	325	163	3
moderate	350	177	4
moderately hot	375–400	190–204	5–6
hot	425	218	7
very hot	450–475	232–245	8–9